DR W GRAHAM SCROGGIE
ON
Luke & John

ARK PUBLISHING
130 City Road, London EC1V 2NJ

CHRISTIAN LITERATURE CRUSADE
Fort Washington, Pennsylvania 19034

Also in this series:
Scroggie on Matthew and Mark
Scroggie on Acts and 1 & 2 Corinthians
Scroggie on Galatians to Jude
Scroggie on The Psalms

©1981 Ark Publishing (UK dist.)
130 City Road, London EC1V 2NJ

Christian Literature Crusade (USA dist.)
Box C, Ft. Washington, PA 19034

First published 1981

ISBN 0 86201 092 6 (UK)
ISBN 0 87508 485 0 (USA)

All rights reserved. No part of this publication may be reproduced, stored in a retrieval system, or transmitted, in any form or by any means, electronic, mechanical, photo-copying, recording or otherwise, without the prior permission of Ark Publishing.

Printed in U.S.A.

Foreword

Dr. Graham Scroggie's works need no introduction. As an outstanding expositor of God's Word and a greatly loved pastor he became widely known, not only in the United Kingdom and the United States of America, but far beyond. His periods as minister of Charlotte Chapel, Edinburgh (1916-1933), and Spurgeon's Metropolitan Tabernacle, London (1938-1944), testify to his powers of preaching and exposition, as week by week he fed crowded congregations with the Word of God.

Dr. Scroggie's gifts found further expression through his participation in Scripture Union's worldwide Bible reading programme. From 1927 to 1931 he was a regular contributor to Daily Notes, a series of expository and devotional readings which brought him into daily contact with hundreds of readers. Those notes are now made available in book form for the first time, not only for those who remember this great Bible teacher, but for all those who will value his clear insight into the enduring lessons of God's Word made personally applicable through the twin gifts of his incisive mind and warm devotion to Christ. Dr. Scroggie's selections are designed to be read together with the Scriptures themselves, to which he regularly turns the reader. His Bible was primarily the King James Version, and his use of this particular text has been consistently retained in the five volumes now published.

Today's reader may wish to follow Scroggie through the Scriptures on a daily basis — each page contains a reading complete in itself — and this was Scroggie's original intention. However, the readings are so designed that one may also move uninterruptedly through each volume without break. They are written as a valuable study and devotional aid and therefore stand in their own right as Bible commentaries to which the reader may turn again and again.

Luke's Gospel

Contents

1:1-17	A surprise for a priest
1:18-38	Unbelief and faith
1:39-56	Two women meet in a crisis
1:57-66	Birth of the Baptist
1:67-80	The Benedictus
2:1-14	Advent of the Saviour
2:15-38	Jesus proclaimed and manifested
2:39-52	Thirty years in summary
3:1-14	The message of John
3:15-23	An end and a beginning
4:1-15	The fortieth day
4:16-32	The lesson reader
4:33-44	The miracle worker
5:1-16	Supplies and disease
5:17-26	Paralysis paralysed
5:27-39	Jesus' defence
6:1-16	Keeping the Sabbath by breaking it
6:17-35	The kingdom sermon
6:36-49	Light on life
7:1-17	The servant and the son
7:18-35	John again
7:36-50	A challenging contrast
8:1-15	Soul soils
8:16-25	Truth and trial
8:26-39	A miracle on a maniac
8:40-56	Twelve years
9:1-11	Pilgrim preachers
9:12-22	Wonderful deeds and words
9:23-36	Cross and crown
9:37-48	Mountain and valley
9:49-62	Three lessons
10:1-12	Missionaries
10:13-24	Flashes of light
10:25-42	In public and in private
11:1-13	How to pray
11:14-26	Springs of action
11:27-44	Plain speaking
11:45-54	Woes for the wicked

12:1-15	Fault, fear and faith
12:16-34	Put God first
12:35-48	The Lord's return
12:49-59	Warning and rebuke
13:1-17	Goodness and severity
13:18-35	Kingdom truths
14:1-14	Feast lessons
14:15-24	The great refusal
14:25-35	Conditions of discipleship
15:1-10	Sensibly and insensibly lost
15:11-32	Brothers apart
16:1-18	What sinners can teach saints
16:19-31	Character and destiny
17:1-10	Christian ethics
17:11-25	Negligence
17:26-37	Coming judgement
18:1-17	How to pray
18:18-30	A poor rich man
18:31-43	The blind beggar blessed
19:1-10	Up a tree
19:11-27	A pound apiece
19:28-40	Palm Sunday
19:41-48	Sad sights
20:1-18	Battle at close quarters
20:19-36	Talk traps
20:37-47	A poser
21:1-13	Forecasts
21:14-24	AD 70
21:25-38	Prophetic signs
22:1-13	A cursed contract
22:14-23	Two feasts
22:24-38	Rebuke, condemnation and warning
22:39-53	The betrayal
22:54-71	Pretentious folly
23:1-12	The Roman trials
23:13-25	Verdicts
23:26-43	The road and the hill
23:44-56	The end
24:1-12	The empty tomb
24:13-24	Three talk
24:25-35	Self-revealed
24:36-53	In, out and up

Introduction

Luke's Gospel

Tradition unanimously declares Luke to be the author of both the third Gospel and the Acts, and while his name does not appear in either treatise, the internal evidence is in harmony with this external testimony. His interest in medical matters as a physician is evident in the narrative (4:23,38; 5:12; 8:43; 13:11; 22:44). His literary style offers constant tribute to his level of culture and education, and the thoroughness with which he prepared his manuscript (1:1-4) is characteristic of a man trained to think, inquire and select.

While it is not possible to determine the date of this Gospel exactly, a fairly accurate estimate can be made. It preceded the Acts (see Acts 1:1) which does not record events after Paul's two years in Rome (about AD 62). Therefore, in all probability the Gospel was compiled during Paul's detention in Caesarea, when Luke would have had ample opportunity for research, thus giving us a date around AD 60.

The book is written for Theophilus (1:1), apparently a man of considerable importance. That his name is Greek suggests that Luke's selection of material was such that would appeal especially to that section of the Gentile world.

The special emphasis of Luke's Gospel as he tells the life of Jesus lies in his deep concern for all in need. He highlights the Saviour's concern for the welfare of women, so often scorned by Jew and Gentile alike. This revelation of Luke's character confirms Paul's description of him as 'the beloved physician'.

Luke 1:1-17

A surprise for a priest

Luke's record is a priceless piece of literature. The *writer* was a Gentile by birth, and a physician by profession. He became Paul's intimate companion, and he wrote two of the twenty-seven parts of the New Testament.

John lays emphasis on the *deity* of Jesus, hence no genealogy; but Luke lays the emphasis on his *humanity*, hence a detailed account of his birth. Tennyson's words describe this Gospel: 'Thou seemest human and divine, the highest, holiest manhood thou.'

In the **Introduction** (1:1-4) Luke says why he wrote. He was neither the first nor the last to supply a record of Christ's life. He also intimates the plan of his record. It is to be *'in order'* (kathexes), consecutive, chronological, and comprehensive; and so, it begins with the *Annunciation*, and ends with the *Ascension*. The writing is dedicated to a Greek (cf. Acts 1:1).

In the first main division of the record (1:5 to 4:13), are **prophecy** (1:5-56), **fulfilment** (1:57 to 2:7) and **estimate** (2:8 to 4:13). The prediction relates to *John* (1:5-25), and *Jesus* (1:26-56), the forerunner and the Saviour.

Our portion sets forth the time and circumstances of the revelation vouchsafed to Zacharias by Gabriel (5-12), and also, the revelation itself (13-17). Simple and beautiful is the description of this man and his wife (5-7). On the hearth of their hearts lay the ashes of a dead hope (7), but these were soon to be kindled again in the joy of parenthood.

The news came while the priest was at his post (8), and while the people were in prayer (10). Duty and devotion are the best preparations for heavenly visions and voices (11). A probably forgotten prayer was now to be answered (13). A boy was to be born who would bless a multitude (13,14). The nature and power of his mission are announced (15-17). He was to prepare the way for *Christ*, and to do so in the energy of the *Spirit*, by turning men to *God*: a trinitarian mission.

Thought: A situation is never hopeless while God lives.

Luke 1:18-38

Unbelief and faith

Note first **the unbelief of Zacharias** (18-20). Here we must distinguish between his question (18) and Mary's (34). That the one lacked faith, and that the other had it, is evidenced by the reply which the angel gave to each, chastening the one, and confirming the other (20, 35-37). Each of these people was faced with a difficulty: the one with a difficulty of nature (18); the other with a difficulty of circumstance (34). In both cases the promise was fulfilled by the performance of a miracle: in the one case by the stimulation of nature (24), and in the other case, by superseding it (35). Zacharias asked for a sign, and he was given one. For nine months he would be both dumb (20) and deaf (62). Mary did not ask for an evidence, but for an explanation (34).

The second paragraph tells of **the people's surprise** (21,22). Our unbelief robs people of what in faith we could and would have said for their encouragement: '*he could not speak unto them.*'

The third paragraph briefly and beautifully tells of **God's faithfulness** to this couple (23-25). Think of Abram and Sarah, of Manoah and his wife, and of Elkanah and Hannah. God does not always do what he can, but he always does what he wills.

The fourth paragraph gives us **the prophecy concerning Jesus** (26-38). Relate *six* in 26, 36, to *five* in 24. The same angel who went to Jerusalem (8) now goes to Nazareth (26). Mary was betrothed but not married (27), and fulfilment of the promise was vouchsafed during her virginity (34,35).

The virgin birth of Jesus is a fact and truth vital for Christianity. It is impressive that a *doctor* records it: and he may have got it from Mary herself. The angel told Mary that her son would be the long-looked-for Messiah (32,33), and the Saviour of the world (31). He also told her about her kinswoman (36,37). And Mary believed (38), her faith being as divine as the predicted event.

Thought: Open your soul to all that God can do for you.

Luke 1:39-56

Two women meet in a crisis

What a scene! **The maiden visits the matron (39-45).** Why did Mary go to Judea at this time? Read Matthew 1:18,19. To such as she was, scandal was worse than death. To be for three months (56) in a house where she was understood (42,43,45) was heaven on earth to her. Elizabeth mothered the mother of Jesus, and that was the next greatest thing to bearing his forerunner.

Three months before John's birth his mother was *'filled with the Holy Spirit'* (41), and he inherited the blessing (15). What Elizabeth said to Mary was inspired by the Spirit just given (42-45). It is a marvellous utterance! She recognises that this maiden is to be the *mother* of the Messiah: she acknowledged both his divinity and humanity, and before he is born, she submits to his rule (43); and she commends Mary's faith, with a reference, perhaps, to the unbelief of Zacharias (45).

In response to all this is **Mary's hymn of thanksgiving** (46-56), called *The Magnificat, Benedictus, Gloria in Excelsis,* and *Nunc Dimittis.* Mary's great song is framed on Hannah's, and is in four strophes: verses 46-48; 48-50, 50-53; 54, 55. It follows the device of Hebrew parallelism; and it reveals not only a pious but also a poetic soul. This latter quality was inherited in a measure by her sons James and Jude (see their writings).

Throughout the song God's *might* and *mercy* are magnified, and in the Christian view, he is never so mighty as when he is merciful to the weak and humble, and never so merciful as when he is mighty against the strong and proud (51-53). Ungodly strength is weakness and God-fearing weakness is strength. Salvation is historically organic (55).

Mary *'returned to her own house'* strong in faith, courageous, and expectant, a lily that no slander could soil.

Thought: Cultivate a clear conscience and be content.

Luke 1:57-66

Birth of the Baptist

This portion records *the birth, circumcision and naming of the Baptist*. The first thing that must impress the attentive reader is the exact detail here presented: the gathering of the neighbours, the proposed name, the mother's decision, the remonstrance, the signs made to the deaf father, the writing tablet and stylus, the father's recovery of speech and hearing, the joy and fear, the report and wonder. Surely all this could have come only from the parties concerned. Read again the introduction (1-4). When Zacharias came home deaf and dumb (23), he must have informed his wife of all that had taken place *by writing it down*: which explains verse 60. The first use the father made of his loosened tongue was *to praise God*. The last thing he had said was not to his credit (18).

Well, a boy was born. No doubt he looked like all other babies, except to his mother's eyes; yet a great soul had been sent into the world; the greatest born of women, the last of the long line of Hebrew prophets, and the forerunner of the Messiah. The greatest personalities in human history have generally been of humble origin. Think of Bunyan, Luther, and others. The true aristocracy are they of moral worth; the nobility are they who do nobly.

Circumcision in Israel was the manifest admission of the child into the visible covenant relationship with God. See Genesis 17:12, Leviticus 12:3.

There are two Bible names which have been freely appropriated by over sixty generations: *John* and *Mary*. Is it not significant that the name *Jesus* has not been appropriated?

We should learn from Zacharias' affliction that unbelief stints our ears towards God, and our mouths towards men; that a Christian's loss is not penal but disciplinary; and that recovery should prove that we have learned our lesson. What a home these three made! A home is vastly more than a house.

Thought: Always follow your own convictions.

Luke 1:67-80

The Benedictus

Like the Magnificat, this utterance is a mosaic of quotations from the Old Testament. Mary's song connects the *praise* of Old Testament and New Testament, and Zacharias' message connects the *prophecy* of both Testaments. Observe that all these are inspired by the Holy Spirit (41,42,67, 2:25-32). Only God knows the future and only by God can anyone else know it. This is a thing very different from the inspiration of Milton, Shakespeare, and others. This great utterance begins on the note *blessed*, and ends on the note *peace* (68,79). The **Benedictus**, as to form, is cast in the mould of Hebrew prophecy, and is in five parts.

The first (68-70) tells of the resumption of prophetic revelation, which had been suspended since the time of Malachi.

The second (70-72) tells of the purpose and work of the coming Messiah. Salvation is his great work: and of what it consists is defined in verses 74,75. Verse 72 has been thought to contain a reference after the manner of the ancient prophets (Isaiah 8:3; Micah 1:10-15) to the name of the speaker, Zacharias —whom the Lord *remembers*; his wife, Elizabeth—the *oath* of my God; and the child, John—the Lord be *merciful*. Note these three words in verses 72,73.

The third paragraph (73-75) connects the work of the Messiah with the Abrahamic covenant, and defines salvation as consisting *outwardly* in deliverance from enemies and *inwardly* in holiness and righteousness of life.

The fourth (76,77) relates John to the Messiah, and defines the former's mission. John is to be *the prophet of the highest* (76). Jesus was *the son of the highest* (32). Compare also *the power of the highest* in verse 35. Only God can give salvation, but we can give the *knowledge* of it (77).

The fifth paragraph (78,79) tells of the need and means of salvation. Godet says that the illustration used is that of pilgrims lost at night in the desert being guided by the rising of a star.

Thought: Get ready for what God wants you to do.

Luke 2:1-14

Advent of the Saviour

The birth of Jesus (1-7). It has been said that there was no such *census decree* as Luke speaks of, but proof of the objection has not been forthcoming. The date of Jesus' birth was probably about 5 BC. By this event *Bethlehem* (house of bread) has been for ever made sacred. Joseph and Mary were married at this time (5, see Matthew 1:20). By a comparison of verse 6, with 1:36,39,56,57, we gather that Jesus was about six months younger than John.

The town was crowded on account of the census order, and Joseph and Mary, being too late to secure accommodation in a hostelry had to put up in a stable, which in all likelihood was a limestone grotto. There, the Saviour of the world was born. A protracted controversy has circled round whether or not Mary had any other children. I believe that those named in Mark 6:3 were all hers, but *'firstborn'* here (7) does not prove anything either way.

The angels and the shepherds (8-14). This section is very full and rich. Mark, specially, *the angel and the angelic host* (9,13); the fact that this revelation was vouchsafed to humble men, and while they were performing their duty (8); their fear, and the exhortation not to fear (9,10); that an angel was the first preacher of the gospel (10); the scope of it, *to all*; the effect of it, *great joy* (10); the substance of it—*Saviour, Christ, Lord*. The human Jesus and the divine Lord met in Christ. This is a declaration of profoundest theological significance.

Compare the *glory* (9) with the *manger* (12). Hear the angelic host sing the *Gloria In Excelsis*, and mark its triple parallelism (14). No cathedral was ever more sacred than that field. The sanctuary is where God meets people.

Thought: Christ's journey was from the glory, by the stable and cross, to the throne.

Luke 2:15-38

Jesus proclaimed and manifested

● **The shepherds and Jesus (15-20).** These shepherds had more insight and understanding than many theologians have, for they recognised that the message of the angels was the Word of the Lord (15). Their *haste* betokens their earnestness (16); and at once they become evangelists (17). No one has any right to keep good news to himself. If you do not tell others of Christ, either you have never known him, or you are unspeakably mean. Listen, see, go, tell—that is the order. It is not for us to *create* the story, but to *communicate* it (17). Mary was a wonderful mother, and contemplated her firstborn with adoring wonder (19,51).

● **The circumcision and presentation of Jesus (21-24).** Compare the former of these events with John's (1:59-63): no family gathering here (21). Forty days later two legal ceremonies were performed. First the purification offering of the mother was brought, and in the case of poor people, a pigeon was substituted for the lamb (24). Second, a firstborn male child had to be ransomed (22,23). This applied to Jesus, who became identified with the law of circumcision (21). This identification of Christ with men is of profoundest significance, making possible our identification with him.

● **Two old saints see the babe Jesus (25-38).** The first of these was *Simeon*. Mark how he is characterised (25); just, devout, expectant, Spirit-endowed. Great emphasis is laid on the last particular: he was not only *endowed* but also *instructed* and *guided* by the Holy Spirit. Are you? Of all who took Jesus in their arms, probably no one but Simeon knew who he was. What he knew by revelation is embodied in his *Nunc Dimittis* (29-32), the fifth of the Lucan songs. It is in three strophes, and is an Old Testament mosaic, as are the *Magnificat*, and the *Benedictus*.

Thought: Illumination is not sudden but gradual.

Luke 2:39-52

Thirty years in summary

In verses 29-32 we have what Simeon said to God about Jesus, and in verses 34,35, what he said to Mary and Joseph. Well might these marvel at what this man had said (33). Observe it does not say that 'his father and mother marvelled' but *Joseph and his mother* (cf. verse 43). This is part of the evidence for the virgin birth which Luke believed to be a fact. Simeon, by inspiration, discloses the mission of Jesus (34,35). Christ is not only a revelation; in revealing God he also reveals us (35).

Anna lived ninety-one years from the time of her marriage, so that she must have been much over a hundred years old at this time (36). See how she spent her time (37). She was the first woman to bear testimony to Christ the Redeemer (38).

Verses 39,40, cover a period of twelve years, the most impressionable years of a child's life. This **summary of Jesus' childhood** is of very great importance, showing, as it does, that he was really human and yet truly divine. *Filled with wisdom* cannot mean that from the beginning he had all wisdom, because in verse 52 we are told that he *increased in wisdom* as he did in stature: but at no stage did his progress imply or prove fallibility.

The next section tells of **Jesus' first visit to the Temple**, i.e. after infancy (42-51). It is the only incident on record of his first thirty years of life (3:23). Compare Jesus' first and last passovers (41, ch.22:14-20). Observe that Jesus was not *teaching* the doctors of the law in the Temple, but listening to them, and answering their questions. Verses 48,49, are wonderful, telling of the reticence which had been observed in the Nazareth home (48), and also of the divine self-consciousness of Jesus at this time (49). Compare Jesus' first and last recorded words.

Thought: It was never intended that divine relations should dishonour human relations.

Luke 3:1-14

The message of John

Frames are for the sake of pictures, and not pictures for the sake of frames. Here verses 2b-18, are the picture: verses 1-2a, are the historical frame. What mattered and matters to the human race is not Caesar, or Pilate, or Herod, or Philip, or Lysanias, or Annas, or Caiaphas, but *John the Baptist*. He had no temporal authority, but he had spiritual power.

The substance of this man's message is given in verses 3-9, from which we learn that it was based on the Old Testament (4-6), that it was a ministry of preparation (4), and that its appeal was to the conscience rather than to the intellect (3,8,9). We badly need another John, a man who out of a holy passion will show us again the axe (9): for, remember, it is still true that all fruitless trees shall be '*hewn down and cast into the fire*' (9). As long as there is *sin* there will be the need for *repentance*, and until there is repentance there can be no *salvation* (6). John's baptism and Christian baptism must not be confused (3,7).

Notice that, arising out of this preaching, certain groups made inquiries of the prophet; *people* generally (10), *tax-gatherers* (12), and *soldiers* (14). Each asked concerning his *duty*. Yes, *duty*. Christianity is not another word for morality, but Christianity is always severely ethical. If you are not ethical, you are not Christian. John warns all against *selfishness* (11), *dishonesty* (13), *violence, false accusation*, and *mutiny* (14). Are these sins obsolete?

It is too generally assumed today that church attenders are Christians. That is a big assumption. Just because there is so little faithfulness in preaching about sin and sins, there is so little conviction and conversion. In the parable the barren soil was to be *digged and dunged*, and there is no use in dunging it until it is digged. In like manner the law prepared for the gospel. In like manner John prepared for Jesus. Let us hold in grateful remembrance the servants of God in days gone by.

Thought: Faithfulness and flattery can never be friends.

Luke 3:15-23

An end and a beginning

Verses 15-18 tell of the impression which the Baptist's ministry had made on the people, and of how he corrected their misconceptions. John was so different from all others that they began to think that he was the long-promised Messiah. Do we so live as to remind people of Christ? When John learned of this surmise he immediately and emphatically put an end to it. He was nothing if not honest, but John was glad to be the slave of Jesus. He contrasts his own and Jesus' ministry. Both came to baptise, John in water, Jesus in Spirit and fire (16).

John's estimate of Jesus, and insight into his purpose and method are wonderful (17). This illustration, taken from eastern agricultural life, is frequently employed. The beaten sheaves, the thrown grain and chaff, the blown chaff, and the garnered grain (17). That represents Christ's purpose and method. Reality and unreality, truth and falsehood, right and wrong, must be separated.

Verses 19,20, are not in their historical order, for what is said in verses 21,22, preceded the imprisonment of John. This great man was no respecter of persons. His eye flashed and his tongue burned in the presence of the sensuous tetrarch, though he must have known that he was likely to pay for his courage with his neck, which he did. A man's beliefs should always be more to him than is his body. Herod was a fool to suppose that he could silence his conscience, or stay the truth, by putting John in prison.

Study carefully the record of Jesus' baptism (21,22). This enduement was for the coming service. If Christ needed it, do not we? Three times God spoke to Jesus: verse 22; Mark 9:7; John 12:28. Trace references to Christ *praying* (21).

Thought: Encourage courage.

Luke 4:1-15

The fortieth day

Note the following facts.

1. Jesus must have told his disciples what had happened, or they could not have put it on record.

2. Luke puts second what Matthew puts first: but almost certainly Matthew's order is chronological, for we cannot think of an attack after Jesus' *'Get thee behind me, Satan.'*

3. This diabolical assault came after the divine attestation: the devil came after the Dove. Times of spiritual triumph are followed by times of severe temptation.

4. The temptation lasted for forty days, and was not only on the fortieth day. Think about that. This record says nothing of the thirty-nine days of struggle, but Jesus faced them. Do not we feel that we do better in a great field day than we do in the humdrum days of petty temptations? Jesus won all through.

5. On the fortieth day were three great assaults, each making a different appeal. The first (2,3) appealed to physical need: the second (5-7) appealed to consciousness of authority and power: and the third (9-11) appealed to an attitude of trust. The danger of these temptations is in that, up to a point, Jesus was asked to do what it was right he should do, and what he was destined to do. He must satisfy his hunger; he must rule the world; and he must trust God. But he was asked to do right things in wrong ways, and from wrong motives. That is the point. Many who are never tempted to do what is gross, are tempted to do what is good in a wrong way.

6. How did Jesus win? *'By the sword of the Spirit, which is the word of God.' 'It is written . . . it is said'* (4,8,12). The Spirit and the Word are invincible against Satan. If we learn to use the Word and let the Spirit use us, we shall be *more than conquerors*.

7. He who *'returned from the Jordan full of the Holy Spirit'* (1) returned in like manner from the wilderness (14). How do you return from temptation?

Thought: The Christian life is a conflict, not a concept.

Luke 4:16-32

The lesson reader

Luke omits between 4:13 and 4:14 a period of fourteen months, the record of which is in John 1:29 to 5:47.

To use modern language, Jesus went regularly to church (16). Distinguish between the Temple and synagogue. The latter originated, probably, in the time of the Babylonian captivity. This synagogue was in Jesus' native town, Nazareth. To witness in one's own home and town is not often easy.

Jesus read from the scroll of Isaiah the lesson appointed for the day. It was in chapter 61. The reading is terminated abruptly at *'the acceptable year of the Lord'* (18,19), omitting *'the day of vengeance of our God'*. Only of what Jesus had read could he say, *'This day is this scripture fulfilled in your ears'* (21). This is still *'the acceptable year'*; *'the day of vengeance'* has not yet come. The passage quoted summarises Christ's mission and message. He came *to preach*, and his message told of *good news, healing, deliverance, vision, liberty, a coming jubilee*.

His brief interpretation and application of this lesson (21) astonished his townsfolk. First they wondered, and then they cavilled (22). Jesus' reply to them reveals their spirit and attitude (23-27), and at last they themselves reveal it (28,29). *'He came unto his own world and his own people received him not'* (John 1:11).

Jesus' illustrations are impressive. He says that of old two distinguished prophets were accepted by *Gentiles*, a woman (25,26), and a man (27), implying that though his own people rejected him, despised foreigners would accept him (24). This filled them with wrath (28). It is said that 'familiarity breeds contempt'. It seemed to do so here (22b). But this carpenter was the Christ, and the hands that bled for you and me on the wood, were none the less worthy because they had worked with wood. Christ has for ever ennobled and sanctified the common task and toil for men.

Thought: Stand up to what it is hardest to endure.

Luke 4:33-44

The miracle worker

Jesus left the people who did not want him, and went to Capernaum by the lake side. He continued to attend the synagogue and to preach (31,32). Opposition did not promote inactivity: challenge only revealed courage. Well, the devil was in church (33). He often is, but sometimes he works silently. On this occasion he disturbed the service.

There is no use saying that in that day men attributed to demon-possession what today medical science knows was something else. The matter is settled by the fact that *Jesus* believed that people were demon-possessed, *and he knew*. Doctors, in this enlightened age, do not always diagnose aright, and that may easily be attributed to something else which is in reality demon-possession. Observe that in verse 34 the man and the demon are identified, *we, us*; and surely it is the demon that says, '*I know thee.*' They have much knowledge who have not all knowledge. Once it was, '*If thou be the Son of God*' (3): now it is, '*I know . . . thou art the Holy One of God*' (34). It is a pity that men deny the deity of Christ when demons acknowledge it. Jesus demonstrates his authority over evil spirits by commanding this one to quit, which it did (35).

We learn that Peter was married, and that his mother-in-law lived with him. She was down with typhus fever – that's what Luke the doctor means by *great* – and Jesus instantly cured her. Diseases as well as demons had to do his bidding. This is shown again in the next paragraph (40,41).

This had been a busy day, and after a short sleep Jesus went to a quiet place among the hills to pray (42-44, see Mark 1:35-39). The greatest argument for prayer is that Christ prayed. But he never was left alone for long, nor did he ever complain of being disturbed. His strength was not dependent upon acts of devotion, but upon an attitude of soul.

Thought: Action and contemplation should never be divorced.

Luke 5:1-16

Supplies and disease

Of this miracle consider the circumstances, the catch, and the consequences.

● **The circumstance** (1-3). Three factors here combine: *the curious crowd, the weary workers,* and *the tireless Teacher.* It was morning and these fishermen were *washing* their unprofitable nets (2,5). *Casting, dragging, washing, mending* — that is the history of nets (Mark 1:16; John 21:8; Luke 5:2; Mark 1:19). Is that your procedure in service? Take time to be efficient. Well, Jesus borrowed a boat and made a pulpit of it, and then he paid for the loan.

● **The catch** (4-7). Four points here should be marked. First, *failure* (5). It had been a bad night. Second, *faith* (4,5). The Carpenter told the fishermen what to do, and though the instructions were contrary to the usual procedure, they acted upon them. *Nevertheless* is the great word here. If none of your actions proceed from a *nevertheless* they will always fall short of being heroic. Third, *fullness* (6). Christ is no man's debtor, and his payments are always profuse. Compare the catch in John 21. Fourth, *fellowship* (7). Supplies sometimes reveal selfishness, but not here. Indeed, had Simon and Andrew not called James and John, they probably would have lost the whole catch. Blessing is secured by being shared: often it is lost by being selfishly held.

● **The consequences** (8-11). These men were thrice called: first, to *discipleship* (John 1:35-44); second, to *service*, here; and third, to *apostleship* (6:12-16). Contact with Christ promotes consciousness of sin (8), but it does not end at that, as the next paragraph shows.

● **Deliverance from a deadly disease** (12-16). Mark this man's *state*, his *opportunity*, his *prayer* (12), his *cure*, his *charge*, and his *disobedience* (14,15; Mark 1:45). Christ's interests are mostly promoted by speech, but sometimes by silence (14).

Thought: See in every difficulty an opportunity.

Luke 5:17-26

Paralysis paralysed

The mosaic of Jesus' ministry is made up of *certain* days, places, circumstances and people (12,17). The scene here is a house, which was crowded, because Jesus was therein, teaching and healing.

The friends of a paralysed man think that Jesus can heal him if only they can get to him. Their desire stirs their ingenuity. As the orthodox way is blocked, they take an unconventional way. No one should be eccentric for eccentricity's sake, neither should any be conventional for conventionality's sake. The great thing is to get to Christ, by whatsoever means.

Observe, it is not the faith of the paralytic that Jesus sees, but that of his friends (20), and because of that, he is healed. For how much does the faith of one man count in the salvation of another?

Notice that it is this man's spiritual need which Jesus first supplies (20). Forgiveness is always the thing of prior importance, just because the eternal is always greater than the temporal, and the spiritual than the physical. Do you believe that?

Well, because good was being done, opposition appeared (21). Too often the official custodians of true religion have been its readiest critics. Certainly if Jesus was not God, he was speaking blasphemy: but if these men had had the spiritual insight and sympathy which their profession implied, they would have known that Jesus was the Messiah. In verse 23, the emphasis is on *to say*. Both these things were equally easy *to say*, and equally hard *to do*. Jesus proved that he had performed the inward by performing the outward miracle (24). Belief in Christ must be based on evidence, for faith is neither ignorance nor credulity; and the evidence is superabundant.

This miracle produced in the people *wonder*, *fear*, and *praise* (26). Christ is still forgiving sins, and by his action proves his Person. What a number of paralysed Christians there are! If *you* are suffering from a stroke, cry now to the Saviour.

Thought: Christ can straighten what is crooked.

Luke 5:27-39

Jesus' defence

This is a singularly full portion. First, there is *Levi's call and feast* (27-32). *Publican* means tax-gatherer, and a Jewish publican was a renegade. Jesus was and always is after bad people, and for the reason here given (31,32). Levi had no goodness to defend, but he wanted to be good. He had heard many voices of condemnation, but when he heard this voice of invitation, *he arose and followed*. Almost at once he became a missionary, and to his own class (29).

Visualise that company with Jesus as chief guest! The scribes and Pharisees had all graduated MM — masters of murmuring (30). Two groups of people were puzzled by Jesus' conduct: these MMs and John's disciples (33, Matthew 9:14). Jesus' reply to the former is classic (31,32). He did not imply that any were *whole or righteous*, but that some thought they were, and so missed the blessings of *health* and *forgiveness*.

So secondly — we see **Jesus questioned about fasting** (33-39). Evidently the feast was on a fast day occasioning the inquiry, in reply to which Jesus says four things.

First, *sorrow does not become a present living fellowship* (34,35). *Taken away* implied a violent death. There come to us all times when sorrow is fitting, but it should never be artificially imposed.

Second, *Christianity was never designed to patch up Judaism* (36): it is an entirely new garment. Such a use of it would spoil Christianity, would be incongruous on Judaism, and would only show the latter's inferiority. Consider carefully these points.

Third, *to combine Christianity with Judaism would be to destroy both* (37,38). The new wine would burst the old wineskins, as the new patch would tear the more old garment.

Fourth, *it is natural to cling to custom and tradition* (39), but it is not always right so to do. The new garment, wine-skin and wine of Christianity are inevitable.

Thought: There is no congruity in compromise.

Luke 6:1-16

Keeping the Sabbath by breaking it

In our first paragraph (1-5), Jesus has something to say on **breaking and keeping the Sabbath**. These Pharisees did not see so far. They did not question the right of the disciples to pass through that field, nor charge them with dishonesty for plucking the ears of corn. What in their view was wrong was that they did the latter *on the Sabbath day*. Jesus answered their question by a question (3,4).

What is common to the two circumstances is not the *Sabbath*, but *hunger*, and Jesus shows that a physical necessity should have precedence over a legal institution. Both David and these disciples were hungry, and so they ate. If it is wrong to eat on the Sabbath, can it be right to live on the Sabbath? Jesus makes a great claim for himself in verse 5. The law-maker is greater than the law, and is the best interpreter of it.

The next paragraph (6-11) is on the same subject, but relative to **the restoration of dexterity**. A useless *right* hand was made serviceable again; atrophy gave way to action. This also was done on the Sabbath; and what better day? But these short-sighted hyper-legalists were on Jesus' track. These men broke the law to defend it, as Jesus showed by his question answer (9). They had no desire that this man should be healed on the Sabbath, yet on that day, they had a desire that Jesus should be killed (11)! About all Jesus' utterances are the notes of sanity and finality.

Now comes **the call of the missionaries** (12-16); twelve of them, and one a devil! What a mystery! No wonder Jesus spent the whole preceding night in prayer (12). What rapture and anguish must have been his that night! What vistas of shame and triumph he must have seen! Summarise the story of each of these men in half-a-dozen lines. Also, collect Christ's prayers, his teaching on prayer, and the occasions of his praying.

Thought: Jesus can put squint eyes straight.

Luke 6:17-35

The kingdom sermon

Luke does not contradict Matthew (17, Matthew 5:1). This *plain* was not in the valley, but was a plateau on the hillside. Easily might Jesus have repeated in various places what he had previously said, but there can be little doubt that this is the sermon recorded more fully in Matthew 5-7. **The occasion and circumstances** are set forth in verses 17-19, and show how widely representative a crowd heard this discourse, and were healingly blessed.

The sermon is here summarised, and may be divided into three parts: *Those who are eligible and ineligible for the kingdom* (20-26); *the principles which characterise the kingdom and to the adoption of which its subjects are called* (27-45); *the supremacy of Christ in his kingdom and the end of the obedient and the disobedient* (46-49).

● **Those who are eligible and ineligible for the kingdom** (20-26). In the first of these parts are two classes of people, those who are blessed (20-23), and those who are not (24-26), and in each is a fourfold discrimination.

The Beatitudes are pronounced upon *the poor, the hungry, the sad, and the persecuted*; and the Woes are pronounced against *the rich, the full, the jolly and the popular*. Now, the interpretation of these clauses needs the most careful safeguarding. The sermon must be regarded in its completeness.

● **The principles which characterise the kingdom and to the adoption of which its subjects are called** (27-45). In the second of the above parts (27-45), Jesus shows that *love is the fundamental principle of his kingdom* (27-30). Its *active* (27,28) and *passive* aspects (29,30) are illustrated. On the one part we should endeavour, and on the other, we should endure.

The Golden Rule (31) is the sum of the law and the prophets. The grand superiority of Christian love over every other moral quality is intimated in verses 32-35. It lives, not by getting, but by giving. Such love is akin to God's and is derived only from him.

Thought: There is no finality of Christian attainment.

Luke 6:36-49

Light on life

We are still in the second part of this great sermon – **the principles which characterise the kingdom, and to the adoption of which its subjects are called** (27-45). In this portion we are told *how love will act in various relations and responsibilities* (36-45). It will be merciful (36), just (37), and generous (38). Mercy and justice are not the same thing, and while neither should be practised at the expense of the other, we should exhibit both.

Judge not must be understood relatively, not absolutely. We all must judge, but what matters is how we do so. Again, we should not *give* in order that we may *get* abundantly (38). Such a motive would vitiate the act. If we do not see, we cannot lead (39): if we are not like Christ in our character, we shall not be Christlike in our conduct (40). Our attitude towards the failings of others goes a long way to reveal ourselves. The hypocrite and self-righteous magnify the faults of others, and minimise their own; yet, often the fact is that the *beam* is criticising the *mote*. He who cannot or will not help himself is not likely to be of much service to others (41,42).

Verses 43-45 carry on the same theme under a different figure. The good or corrupt fruit is the effect of one man's influence on another. Everything in the moral as in the physical realm is *after its kind*. Root and fruit agree.

● **The supremacy of Christ in his kingdom, and the end of the obedient and the disobedient** (46-49) summarises the third part of this great sermon. He himself is the basis of his kingdom. To build on him is to abide; to build on anything else is to perish. Christianity does not consist in the profession of it, but only in the practice of it (46). Words should correspond with deeds; when they do not, a man's life is not only a disharmony, but also a disease.

Thought: Better be a crow than a chameleon.

Luke 7:1-17

The servant and the son

Here are two miracles: one on a Gentile, and the other on a Jew; one on a slave, and the other on a son; one performed at a distance, and the other on the spot; one on behalf of an owner and the other for a mother; one by request, and the other unsolicited; one delivering from death, and the other, delivering from the dead; the one at Capernaum, and the other at Nain.

The servant healed (1-10). *Dear* (2) expresses *value* rather than *affection*; the man was a slave. This centurion must have been a Jewish proselyte. The ruins of his synagogue have been unearthed, and can be seen today. This soldier was a gentleman, and had formed a high opinion of Jesus: the one point is reflected in his procedure (3,6,7), and the other, in his message (6-8). He believed that Jesus had the power in the moral realm which he himself had in the military. This belief in Jesus' *authority* is truly wonderful in this man, at that time; so wonderful that Jesus *marvelled* (9). Here he did so at *belief*, and only once again, but at *unbelief* (Mark 6:6). I wonder what the slave thought about it! Jesus blesses some at the request of others, therefore pray.

The son raised (11-17). This, as we judge, is a much greater event than the former. The slave was the centurion's convenience, but the son was the mother's subsistence: the one rose from his bed, but the other came out of Hades. Sickness and death being the products of sin, Jesus is the enemy of both. In the former miracle we see Jesus' *care*, but in the second, his *compassion*. He is ever the helper of the helpless. His power was and is controlled by his love, and his love found expression alike in word (*weep not*) and deed (*touched the bier*). This is the first time that Jesus raised the dead (compare the other two occasions). Elijah-like, he was Elijah's Lord.

Thought: Look to Christ for life and health.

Luke 7:18-35

John again

Jesus muzzles John (18-23). The Baptist was in prison at Machaerus in Perea. Clearly he was allowed visitors, and when some of his disciples told him of Jesus' miracles, doubt caused him to wonder (18,19). His prison must have been very depressing, and depression weakens faith and strains patience. John gives evidence of both effects. He who had said, *'There standeth one among you whose shoe's latchet I am not worthy to unloose; behold the Lamb of God,'* now asks, *'Art thou he?'*

More people live in mountains and valleys than on plains: experience is much up and down.

Well, Jesus did not blame John. His answer was not in words, but in deeds (21-23). What Christianity accomplishes is its true apologetic. A sinner saved is worth more than all our arguments. Jesus did not say plainly to John, as he did to the Samaritan woman, that he was the Messiah, but he supplied the evidence which would shut John up to that conclusion. I doubt not that this much needed encouragement had the desired effect upon this man's spirit.

And now, **Jesus estimates John** (24-30). He was more than a reed, more than a courtier, more than a prophet. He was the greatest of the prophets and the last of them. The greatest, because foretold, and because he was Jesus' forerunner (27). But Christ declares that the least disciple in the new dispensation is in relation and privilege greater than the greatest of the preceding age, though not necessarily so in moral and spiritual attainment.

In what follows, it is shown that that generation would have **neither John nor Jesus** (31-35). All righteous testimony is rejected by some people, whether it be clothed in gravity or gladness, weeping or laughing; they will not have it. This only shows that one must be *inside* to understand (35). Obedience brings insight.

Thought: There is insight inside.

Luke 7:36-50

A challenging contrast

Jesus accepted invitations of a social character (36). He did not cut himself off from the innocent joys of the people, any more than he did from their inevitable sorrows. What a guest to have at one's table! In the light of Simon's character (44-46), one wonders why he invited Jesus to his house: and, still more, one wonders why Jesus went. But he who foreknew this man's negligence, foreknew also this woman's need, and so he suffered the one to supply the other.

Right in the middle of the narrative is an incomparable parable, peculiar to Luke. It is set forth in twenty-four words in Greek, but how profound and far-reaching is its teaching! (41,42a). It links together the two parts of the story.

What a contrast this man and this woman present! A Pharisee, a harlot; well-to-do, poor; respected, despised; self-righteous, conscious of sin; haughty, humble; dry-eyed, tearful; neglectful, worshipful; patronising, loving; unbelieving, trustful; insensible, repentant; guilty, forgiven. And the difference is made by the attitude of each to Christ.

Let us not lose sight of the fact that Jesus never stood upon ceremony, and never sacrificed fairness for formality. Though he was this man's guest, yet he spoke to him words of plain rebuke. It is a difficult and delicate thing sometimes to be perfectly true to God, to others and to oneself at the table of our entertainers. Have you not found that? Some people think more of keeping up a conversation than of maintaining a standard. Do you?

Ethically the man was better than the woman. In the terms of the parable, she owed ten times as much as he did. But if they were *unlike* in their debt, they were *alike* in their bankruptcy. Of what, then, had Simon to be proud? In the parable, Jesus, the creditor, intimates his willingness to forgive *both*, but in the story, only the woman is forgiven. Her love was not the *ground* but the *proof* of her forgiveness. By her faith she was qualified to *go into peace*.

Thought: Shun snivelling servility.

Luke 8:1-15

Soul soils

Verses 1-3 are full of meaning. Mark two things especially. First, **the wide circuit of Jesus' ministry.** He went where the crowd was, into the '*cities*' and also where scattered groups of peasants were to be found, the '*villages*'. The tremendous importance and necessity of such itinerant evangelism will be apparent, when we remember that China and India are worlds of villages. Christ's mission was not one of Christianisation, but of convert-making.

Second, **Jesus and the ministry of women.** What to us today is a commonplace, was at that time a revolution. When it is recalled what was woman's status in the ancient world, women, above all others, should be grateful for Christianity. The three important details about these women are, that they had all been healed by Jesus, that they were all rich, and that they were grateful enough to be devoted.

Now follows **the great parable of the soils**, with its interpretation (4-15). The sower is one, the seed is one; it is the soils which differ. Study each carefully *the wayside hearer* (5,12); *the rocky-place hearer* (6,13); *the thorny-ground hearer* (7,14); *the good soil hearer* (8,15). Probably each of these types is in every crowd gathered to hear the gospel. Our Lord is not teaching that three-fourths of the scattered seed is lost, for he does not say what proportion of the whole field these first three parts represent. The seed is rendered fruitless in the first case by the *devil*; in the second by the *flesh*; and in the third, by the *world*. The seed comes to harvest in the fourth case because all these three are resisted.

No parable perfectly illustrates all the truth, and so we should remember that the *good ground* hearer does not make himself good. A lot of truth relative to this is not in the parable at all. The call in verse 8b implies *capacity*—ears; *opportunity*—ears to hear; and *responsibility*—let him hear.

Thought: The alternatives are fertility or sterility.

Luke 8:16-25

Truth and trial

The parable of the lamp (16-18) is closely related to what precedes, only under another figure. It is really a parable on parables. What Jesus says is, in effect, that he teaches in parables, not that his disciples only should have the truth, but that, by means of them, it might be given to others.

The reference in verse 17a, has nothing to do with the manifestation of sins in the judgement, but refers to truth diffused as light. This gives point to *therefore* in verse 18. If we have light, we are under an obligation to give it, and if we give it not, it will be extinguished. Not to use, is to lose. Tell what you know. It is a terrible thing when one only *seems to have*.

The next paragraph is on **the new relationship** (19-21). *Brethren* almost certainly means *brothers* — Mary's other sons. What did they want? We are not told, but from Jesus' answer to those around it would appear that they were anxious to draw him away from what he was doing, considering perhaps his need of food and rest. But the time for that sort of solicitude had gone. Christ was about his Father's business. As spiritual interests rise above material concerns, so divine relations are greater than natural ties. By this new law Christ brings a vast multitude of people into relation with himself (21). Are you a relative of God?

The next incident tells of **panic in a storm** (22-25). It was a storm of *wind*, churning up the lake, and causing its waves to flood the boat. Jesus was asleep. He had had a heavy day and was tired. His disciples were afraid. They had some faith, but not enough. Panic led them to talk of perishing, and so they went to their sleeping master. He arose and **rebuked** first the wind, and then them. '*Where is your faith?*' Of what use is a creed that is not available or effective in a crisis? It is to be feared that today it is the disciples that are sleeping in the storm.

Thought: In a tempest it is better to trust than to tremble.

Luke 8:26-39

A miracle on a maniac

Those who look for difficulties in this story can easily find them. A child may ask a question which a philosopher cannot answer. A psychological problem arises at the point where the demons enter into the swine, and an ethical problem in the fact that Jesus allowed them to do so, with the consequent loss to the owners. Relative to the first, we must plead much ignorance; and as to the second, we must remember that if the people lost their swine, they gained security by the healing of this maniac.

What a case this was (27-29)! Such a one is impossible in our country, because, under the influence of Christianity, hospitals and psychiatric units are established for those who are physically, emotionally or mentally sick. There may be a closer connection between some forms of mental illness and demon possession than mental and medical science allows. It is noteworthy that in the Gospel records, the name of God is often on the lips of demons (28). They who torment are afraid of torment. The cruel are cowardly. There is a demon society (30). I wonder how they get on with one another! Why should demons be afraid of water (31)?

By securing their request (32) they were denied their desire (31). But in the case of the man, the refusal of his request (38) was the fulfilment of his desire (38,39). And in the case of the people, both request and desire were granted (37). Distinguish these three carefully, and interpret your prayer, denied or answered, in the light of them.

If, in the presence of Christ, we have not faith, we must have fear (35,37). We either want to be with him, or want him far from us (37,38). Which? What a picture of the sinner this man is! And what a revelation of the Saviour! What a change Jesus can make (29,35)! People who say they do not believe in sudden conversion are only advertising their ignorance. Yes, Christ is able to save to the uttermost.

Thought: Only the forgiven are free.

Luke 8:40-56

Twelve years

Here is a miracle within a miracle, demonstrating Jesus' abundance alike of power and grace. What a heart he had, and has for the lonely, for those whose margin of joy is very narrow.

● **The girl** (41,42,49-56). She was an *only* daughter. This feature is in the other two cases of the conquest of death. The young man was an *only* son, and Lazarus was the *only* brother. These three mark stages of distress; the girl was newly dead, the youth was on the way to the tomb, and Lazarus had been in the grave four days. Yet all were equally dead. By nature we are all spiritually dead, but practically, all are not equally corrupt.

The father came for the daughter. Have you been to Christ about your children? Are they not spiritually sick? Perhaps one or other of them is like Peter, *ready to sink*. Get you quickly to the Saviour about your girl or boy.

Religious associations do not save us from spiritual sickness. This girl's father was ruler of the synagogue. A tremendous strain was put on this man's patience by the delay caused by this woman. Then came the heart-sinking news that she was *gone*. But before the father could speak, Jesus did; note what he said (50).

Now follows the bedroom scene (51-56). Mockers do not see miracles; favour is extended here to faith. What sleep is to us, death was to Jesus.

● **The woman** (43-45). Pour soul! For twelve years she had been very lonely, unfitted for all the relationships of life by her disease; ceremonially unclean. Desperation made her bold. With her, it was now or never. Many jostled Jesus, but she *touched* him. The healing virtue was not in his fringe, not in her faith, though both were instrumental (44,48). Having healed her, Jesus drew her to confess her need and his power. You too may *go into peace* by that door. Will you?

Thought: Dignity is a poor substitute for deliverance.

Luke 9:1-11

Pilgrim preachers

Distinguish between the mission of the *Twelve* referred to here, and of the *Seventy* (10:1-24). The former was towards the end of the second period of the Galilean ministry, and the latter was during the Perean ministry, much later. There came a time in the ministry of the Lord, when he gave the public less, and the Twelve more teaching attention. The reason for this was twofold: first because the public were rejecting him; and second, because he was soon to leave the world, and must train his apostles to carry on the work.

Distinguish between power (*dunamis*) and authority (*exousia*) in verse 1. Either may exist without the other, but Jesus had both, and gave both to his apostles.

Mark the scope and character of the commission: *demons* and *diseases*, *preaching* and *healing*. Relate the first and third, the second and fourth. The Jewish commission is the Christian also. *Preach* here is *kerusso* — to herald, not *evaggelizo* — to proclaim good tidings, though, of course, the news was good.

What follows (3-5) must be carefully interpreted. These men were apostles, not beggars; travellers, not tramps. They were to look to God alone, who would provide for them through people. This essential principle still stands, though conditions and circumstances have greatly changed, and with them, methods of procedure.

Well, they did what they were told (6), and returning, reported their doings (10). By taking these men aside into privacy (10), Jesus teaches the necessity of rest, of quiet time to mend our broken nets. But he teaches also (11) that such rest may, at times, have to be sacrificed.

The lesson in verses 7-9, is that, even the most debased conscience will cry out until it is killed. Read Shakespeare's *Macbeth* again. Conscience is not infallible, but it is against what is wrong every time. Sin is still sin after the lapse of years.

Thought: Sacrificial service is the full flower of love.

Luke 9:12-22

Wonderful deeds and words

There were **two miraculous feedings** (12-17), one in the second, and the other in the third period of Christ's Galilean ministry; one of 5,000, and the other of 4,000 men; one with five loaves and two fishes, the other with seven loaves and a few small fishes; twelve baskets of remains in the one case, and seven baskets in the other case; small *wicker baskets* in the former, and large *rope baskets* in the latter; the one is recorded by all four evangelists, and the other by Matthew and Mark only.

In both cases was the feast conducted in an orderly fashion (14); in both was a blessing asked; and in both did the apostles distribute the meal. In both also, it is said that the people were *filled*.

In each, three lessons are taught: that Jesus regards our temporal need; that he who thus cares for our bodies, cares for and can satisfy the hunger of our souls; and that he himself is the bread which had to be broken before the need of the world could be met.

The next paragraph tells of **the great confession** (18-22). Jesus asked two questions. 'Who am I in the thoughts of the *people*?' 'Who am I in your thoughts, my *apostles*?' The one prepared the way for the other. The guesses of the people were all good, but not good enough (19). Christ is better than the best of men. Evidently all regarded him to be a *prophet*. He was *the* prophet. You cannot fit him into any merely human category, however good.

All the apostles were asked, but one answered (20, cf.Matthew 16:16-19). This is the central point in Jesus' training of the twelve. There had been previous confessions of Christ's deity (John 1:49; 6:69), but nothing so full and emphatic as this, which may be regarded as 'the first adoring confession of the New Testament church'. That question of long ago is still the supreme question: *What do you think of Christ?* It matters, now and for ever.

Thought: There is no confession where there is no conviction.

Luke 9:23-36

Cross and crown

Here is firmly laid **the basis of Christian discipleship** (23-27). It is *absolute surrender to, and utterly devoted following of, Jesus Christ*. *After me . . . follow me*, with nothing between. *Aparneomai* means to disown and renounce. But what? *Self*, the unregenerate and 'unregenerable' self. Have you done that? What then?

Follow Christ, bearing your own cross (23). And this must be done *daily*. Christ is the only one who has the right to ask this of you and me, because he is the only one who has endured the cross for us all. Are you *forsaking* or *following* him?

The Christian life is a sublime anomaly (24). To gain we must lose; to have we must give; to live we must die. Well did Augustine say, '*Let me die, lest I die.*' The *world* and the *soul* can never be of commensurate value (25). No one ever yet has gained *the whole world*, but could one do so at the price of his soul, it would be the most tragic bargain ever struck.

Then, if Christ is the great gain, why should any of us be ashamed of *him* (26), or of his *words*? Is your life a confession of Christ? Remember, there are other ways of denying Christ than by the lips. For every lip-denial there are thousands of life-denials. But as we sow, we shall reap (26b). How tremendous is Christ's claim for himself in verse 26!

Almost certainly verse 27 refers to **the transfiguration** which followed a week later (28-36). What a scene! God, Jesus, Moses, Elijah, Peter, James, John, glory, clouds, sleep, voices, wonder, fear! Jesus' sufferings were placed between glory anticipated and glory realised. No one who is asleep will see Christ's glory (32). Peter never forgot this experience, and in his second epistle he uses, in connection with it, two words he learnt here: *tabernacle* and *decease* (33,31 and 2 Peter 1:13-15, with 16-18). Store great events in your memory.

Thought: Schools are useless unless scholars learn.

Luke 9:37-48

Mountain and valley

How tremendous is the contrast between the scenes on the mountain and in the valley! Peter had been for staying up there (33), but Jesus was needed below. It is true, not only geographically, but also of human experience, that wherever there is a mountain there is a valley. Glory and gloom never lie far apart; joy and sorrow are neighbours; day and night chase one another; action and reaction are common to us all. How desperate would need in the valley be, if help never came from the mountain!

This boy was an *only child*. A one-child family is always an anxiety; yet one is better than none. Children suffer as well as adults, nor does the devil leave them alone.

Is it not so that often the organised church, like these disciples, has displayed complete impotence in the presence of urgent spiritual need? It should not and need not be so. Jesus always was a devil-chaser. How they hate him! But their presence and activities ever reminded him of the solemn work which he had come to do (43,44).

His disciples were expecting him to set up a visible kingdom, and so did not understand his talk about the cross (45). Too often our preconceptions stand in the way of truth. It is easier to anchor in tradition than to pursue truth. Expectation is good only if it is rightly founded. We should expect not for our *wants*, but for our *needs*.

How completely these disciples failed to understand, the next paragraph shows (46-48). And not only were their messianic hopes astray, but also their whole conception of life (46). Jesus here defines true greatness (48). It is never attained along the line of self-importance, but along the line of simplicity and sacrifice. How profound is the teaching here concerning the child, the Saviour, and the Father (48). How rarely is the essential greatness of childhood carried over into maturity!

Thought: It is better to bless than to boss a brother.

Luke 9:49-62

Three lessons

Three important paragraphs claim our attention.

● **Tolerance** (49,50). Here is a man *doing good*, but because he did not belong to the circle of the apostles, John would have stopped him. That is both bigotry and intolerance, and neither becomes a Christian.

The answer which Jesus gave is profound (50). There are believers outside of organised Christianity. That another does not follow 'us' matters little, so long as he follows Christ (49). With Jesus' reply here compare Matthew 12:30. Between verses 50 and 51, place John 7:2 to 10:21.

● **Vindictiveness** (51-56). Here also John figures, together with his brother — both excellent men. But excellent people can make extraordinary mistakes, and exhibit a most unexcellent spirit. Of course it was a thousand pities that these Samaritans did not receive Jesus, but we cannot wonder at it (John 4:9). Even his *own* received him not (John 1:11). Well, these 'sons of thunder' proposed lightning (54); good men, mark you. Racial animosity for a while ruled out Christian charity. Is that never done nowadays?

The occasion led Jesus to define his mission (46). He is not the destroyer, but the deliverer.

● **Discipleship** (57-62). There are three cases. Two offer, and one is invited, but so far as we know, none of them went forward. *Ambition* hindered the first; *insensibility* the second; and *sentimentality* the third. Each wanted to put something other than Christ, *first*. But the unalterable and universal condition of discipleship with him is that always and in all things he must be first.

Read chapter 14:25-33. Test yourself just now by this standard.

Thought: Christ claims absolute proprietorship of you.

Luke 10:1-12

Missionaries

It is important to observe that 9:51 to 18:14 is *peculiar* to this Gospel, that the ministry is chiefly *Gentile* and that it is exercised mainly in *Perea*.

This lengthy section is in three parts. In the first (9:51 to 13:21), **Jesus defines the principles of his kingdom.** In the second (13:22 to 17:10), **Jesus describes the subjects of his kingdom.** In the third (17:11 to 18:14, and on to 19:27), **Jesus declares the coming of his kingdom.**

Chapter 10:1-24 tells of *the mission of the seventy*. Notice that these *seventy* did not include the *twelve*, that they went forth in pairs, and that Christ *followed* them. We do not know the name of one of them. What matters is, that we do our work, not that our names are known. Jesus has taught us the importance of companionship in service by sending out his missionaries by *twos*.

It is good to think that long before Calvary, Jesus had so many who believed in him as to allow of his choosing at least eighty-two for special service, and that after his resurrection he could appear to *above five hundred brethren at once*. His kingdom was established in the world before he left it (9, 11).

Do we share his vision (2a), and his sorrow (2b)? A vast field, but few faithful followers. No one can honestly pray that this work may be done who is not willing to help do it. The apparent hopelessness of the task is indicated by the words — *lambs among wolves*. Yet, after nineteen hundred years, the wolves have not devoured the lambs.

The course followed from Pentecost to now shows that verse 11 is not of universal and permanent application. Paul went back to Lystra (Acts 14:19-23). World evangelisation is not only a privilege, *it is a duty*.

Thought: Help to build the city of God.

Luke 10:13-24

Flashes of light

Christ never put a complexion upon anything which did not belong to it. He never led his followers and missionaries to expect what would not come. He frankly indicated not only coming difficulty, but failure also (10-16). He did this often, in language parabolic as in chapter 8:4-15, and in language plain, as here. What he says in verses 12-15 he had said before, Matthew 11:21-24. The things which the Master said twice, or more often, and there are hundreds of them, should receive special attention.

In this repetition, he teaches two solemn lessons, namely, first, that *privilege is liable to be despised* (15); and second, that *judgement is measured by opportunity* (12-14). The question is often asked, 'What about the heathen who have never heard the gospel?' and the answer is, '*Shall not the Judge of all the earth do right?*' (Genesis 18:25). There are degrees of punishment just because there are degrees of guilt.

These *seventy* had had not a little success, and they were elated (17). Jesus' answer is most impressive. He says three things: first, that in what has been done (17), he sees the potency and prophecy of Satan's overthrow (18); second, that nothing can separate his disciples from him (19); and third, that the roots of their joy should be in their living relation to God, and not in their success in his service (20).

Now follows one of a number of Jesus' prayers which are recorded in the Gospels (21). It is his *Magnificat*. Notice how he addresses God. He claims that his own teaching is *revelation*. He discloses that it was and is *good in the Father's sight* to pass by the worldly wise, and to show his truth to sunny, childlike souls.

Jesus' claims for himself in verse 22 are tremendous. The truth of his prayer (21) is here seen in operation (23, 24).

Thought: See the coming victory in the present struggle.

Luke 10:25-42

In public and in private

Two incidents claim our attention.

- **Jesus and the lawyer** (25-37). We are not to suppose that this man had any evil design in approaching Jesus; the word *tempted* need not have that significance; but, on the other hand, there is no evidence that he was deeply concerned about *inheriting eternal life*. It would appear that his intention in coming was to have 'a trial of wits with the great teacher'.

In answer to his question about the future, Jesus points him to the past (25, 26). He relates *life* to *law*. The inquirer had discernment, for he goes at once to what is vital in the Law — *thou shalt love* (27). Mark carefully Jesus' reply (28). *Do, and live*. But as no one can so do who does not live (spiritually), the clear implication is that we must live in order so to do: that is, we do not love in order to live, but we live in order to love. Cleverly, the lawyer seizes upon the one word in Jesus' reply which gave him the opportunity of carrying on an argument — the word *neighbour* (27, 29).

This drew from the Master the incomparable parable of *the good Samaritan* (30-35). The chief persons are three Jews and a Samaritan. Two of these Jews pass by the third in his need, but the hated Samaritan comes to his help. The neighbour is not the one who needs, but the one who helps (36, 37). Ceremony is a poor substitute for compassion.

- **Jesus and two sisters** (38-42). What it is essential to learn from this is, that service must never be made a substitute for worship, and that worship never draws back from necessary work. Only in the light of these two truths can we understand verse 42. This is not a case of *action versus contemplation*. Mary had been active, but knew when and where to sit down.

Thought: Conduct should be the answer to casuistry.

Luke 11:1-13

How to pray

Here is a great lesson on **prayer**. Jesus prays (1); he teaches his disciples a prayer (2-4); he encourages them to pray by means of a parable (5-8); he assures them of an answer to earnest prayer (9,10); and he appeals to common experience (11-13). The Jews prayed three times a day, at nine, twelve and three o'clock, and, no doubt, verse 1 refers to one of these hours.

The model prayer (2-4) is another of our Lord's repetitions (cf. Matthew 6:9-15, for the full text). Recently I came across this: 'In a certain ancient kirk on the outskirts of Edinburgh, is the following remarkable annotation on the Lord's Prayer. First, we have the highest and most intimate of all relationships, that of son to his father – *Our Father*. Next, we descend to the worshipper in the temple – *Hallowed be thy name*. Coming lower, the citizen in the state – *Thy kingdom come*. Lower still, the servant and his master – *Thy will be done*. Again descending, the beggar in the street – *Give us this day our daily bread*. Continuing the descent, we come to the debtor and his creditor – *Forgive us our debts*. Deepest and lowest of all, the captive in chains – *Deliver us from evil*.'

In this comprehensive prayer every chord in the gamut of human feeling is struck, and from every relationship in which we stand to God and man, ascends to heaven a sharp, short cry.

The following parable is wonderful. Study the **three friends**: one with need, one with supply and one who connects the need and the supply; that is, the world, God and the church. The man who had the supply was very unlike God, who never grudges his gifts. But prayer must be earnest: *ask, seek, knock* – increasing vehemence of entreaty, taken from the parable. We only insult God when we suppose that we are kinder to our dependants than he is to us all in our need (11-13).

Thought: Our knees can carry us further than our feet.

Luke 11:14-26

Springs of action

How often the good which Jesus did was made the occasion of insult and challenge (14,15)! Yet, it is better that our good should be evil spoken of, than that our evil should be well spoken of. It is better to suffer for righteousness' sake, than righteously to suffer for iniquity's sake.

The man Jesus healed had a dumb devil, but the men who commented on the miracle had loquacious devils. Jesus, who made the one man to speak, spoke the other men to silence. There are still sign-seekers in the world (16), but the only sign is the Saviour.

Beelzebub was the *fly-god* of the Ekronites, which the Jews called Beelzebub, the *filth-god*; no greater insult could have been given to Christ, therefore, than these Jews gave him (15). But he answered their insolence with reason (17-19). He illustrates a great principle by reference to a *kingdom*, a *house*, and a *person*, showing that it is applicable always, everywhere. Division brings desolation, and such conflict as this ends in chaos.

Then Jesus turns upon the claims of Jewish exorcists, and argues that if his *reality* is devil-inspired, what is to be said of their pretence (19)? Verses 21, 22, illustrate verse 20. Read *strong one*, not *man* in verse 21. This *strong one* is the devil, the world is his palace, and men's souls are his *goods*. The *stronger one* is Christ, who routs the devil (22).

With verse 23, compare 9:50. These statements do not contradict: they are two tests applied in quite different circumstances. By 9:50, we are to test the judgements we are apt to pass on neighbours; but by 11:23, we are to test our own devotion to Christ.

Jesus goes on to teach that *goodness can never* be merely negative (24-26). No life can for long be *empty*. If good does not fill your soul, evil will.

Thought: Christ calls for our confession, and not our criticism.

Luke 11:27-44

Plain speaking

Sign-seekers have signs enough, if only they have eyes to see them (29-32). It is not more light that we need, but better sight. Two Old Testament illustrations are used to show how heathen received light from abroad, while those who boasted that they were God's people were rejecting God's son.

The Queen of Sheba and the Ninevites are a standing condemnation of the Jews, of that and every time, who reject Jesus. It is here taught that voices of the past shall be heard again in the future (31,32).

Do you believe that there is a judgement to come? Jesus consistently claimed to be greater than the greatest of the past. Do you accept his claim? If you do not you cannot be a Christian, because if he has not spoken the truth he cannot be a Saviour.

Consider carefully verses 33-36. Good lights are of little use to bad eyes; and they are of no use at all if relegated to the basement, or put under a bushel. Candles don't shine through concrete. *Single* in verse 34 must mean *good* because it is contrasted with *evil*. If one's light is darkness, how can one's darkness be light? Yet these Jews thought they knew.

Arising out of this talk, Jesus accepts an invitation to eat in the house of a Pharisee. He was firm in rebuke in another Pharisee's house (7:36-46), but he is withering in his exposure of this man's hypocrisy, and that of his class. He ate of his figs, and called him a *fool*. God hates sham, insincerity, religious formalism, cant, humbug, hypocrisy, feigned piety. At these things he hurls his *woes*. I would rather have a clean soul in a defiled body, than a defiled soul in a clean body; but that is never a necessary alternative. Nevertheless, it is always the inward and not the outward that matters most — always.

Thought: 'Cosmetise' your soul rather than your skin.

Luke 11:45-54

Woes for the wicked

Lawyer in the New Testament, does not mean, as now, one who is versed in or who practises law, but one who interpreted the Jewish traditions. That this class was closely connected with the Pharisees is clear from what this man says (45). He regarded as *reproach* what in matter of fact, was *reproof*, which shows that he was unconvicted and unrepentant. That this is so is evident from Jesus' reply (46-52). He never hurled *woes* at contrite souls.

The reply is addressed to this man's class, whose reputation was nothing to boast of. Christ's first charge against them is that they imposed duties upon the people which God had not required, and which they themselves did not fulfil (46). Those who do that are tyrants, not teachers.

Jesus then charges them with the hypocrisy of concealed hatred (47,48). They venerated the dead, and persecuted the living; they *allowed*, agreed, with former murderers, yet adorned the tombs of their victims. Christ pronounces upon this by a reference to a previous pronouncement (49-51). *The wisdom of God* Godet thinks, is the Book of Proverbs, and that which follows is 'a condensed quotation or paraphrase from Proverbs 1:20-31, in which prophets and apostles are the living organs of the Spirit of God, and their persecution the setting at naught of God's counsel'. For *Abel* see Genesis 4; and for *Zacharias*, 2 Chronicles 24:20-22.

What is said of these lawyers (52) is true also of any person or group that reserves to itself the power and right to interpret the Scriptures, while darkening their plain meaning, and so robbing the people of the light. Observe that the Scriptures are called *the wisdom of God*, and *the key of knowledge*. These wretches waited in vain for some unguarded word from Jesus (53,54). Have others, like them, been equally disappointed in us?

Thought: Light makes worms wriggle.

Luke 12:1-15

Fault, fear and faith

He who had just routed his foes now rallies his *friends* (4), and he addresses them in public (1). This is lateral instruction, and may be very effective in train or tram. *Leaven,* when used figuratively, signifies what is *evil* (1).

Jesus declares that that which hypocrisy covers, shall sooner or later be disclosed: the wickedness which lurks behind forms of worship; the sin which service often hides (3). He then makes an opposite use of verse 2, and declares that the Christian revelation which was vouchsafed and cherished quietly would soon be blazed abroad (3). The full truth is that shame shall be shamed, and truth shall be triumphant.

Attention should be paid to what Christ says about *fear* (4,5). This is a quality which we are in danger of losing, not because we are cultivating courage, but because we are lionising recklessness. To fear physical suffering may be cowardly, but not to fear God is a sin.

The fear spoken of is not *terror,* but is a moral quality which relates itself to moral standards and issues. It is highly compatible with the simplest *trust* (6,7). Five sparrows stuck in a row on a wooden skewer were sold for two farthings. God regarded the one that was *given away.* Then, why should *we* doubt or distrust him?

So to do is to incur solemn consequences (8-10). Confession is rewarded with confession, and denial with denial. In the other records, the *unpardonable sin* is connected with attributing Jesus' saving work to Satanic power, virtually charging him with devilry. They who fear that they have committed this sin prove that they have not by their fear. They who fear God have nothing else to fear (11,12). *Take no thought* does not mean *do not think,* but *do not fret,* be not worried.

Thought: Christ is the test of character.

Luke 12:16-34

Put God first

● **Covetousness** (16-21). We must also consider verses 13-15, for the following parable was occasioned by this interview, and this man is made the text of a sermon on covetousness. This incident is important as showing that in his teaching Jesus stood by principles, and left the detailed application of them to his hearers. The discerner was not a *divider*: he was not a magistrate in a local court, but a revealer of profound principles of conduct, which, if rightly applied, would solve all our problems, domestic, social, industrial.

The all-covering fact and truth is that '*a man's life consisteth not in the abundance of the things which he possesseth*'. Of course not, when you come to think of it. Life is independent of property and dividends. Many without these live gloriously, and many with them fail ignominiously. Life has no more to do with lands than with lip-stick.

Study carefully this parable of *the rich fool*. Up to a point he was right when he said, *My fruits, my barns, my goods, my soul*, but when he began to mortgage *time* (19), he was hopelessly astray.

You and I have only the present moment. What a conception of life is betrayed in *eat, drink and be merry*! A jackass can do that, and they who think of life in such terms are not unlike jackasses. Life is a trust and a probation, and all that any of us will take with us into the other world is what we *are*.

● **True life** (22-34). Jesus shows of what life really consists. The way to the realisation of it is in trustful dependence on God. He who cares for ravens and lilies cannot forget men and women and children (24,28). He does not say that if we pursue the things of the kingdom, God will care for us, but, *because* he cares for us, we should seek first his kingdom (30-32). Have an account in the bank which cannot break (33,34).

Thought: Temporal independence is by spiritual dependence.

Luke 12:35-48

The Lord's return

The record of Luke 11:1 to 17:10 is continuous, unbroken by anything in the other Gospels. We should endeavour, therefore, to see the relation to one another of its various parts. These verses are about *Christ's second coming*.

Those who believe that his coming is only spiritual and continuous will have difficulty with this discourse. If Christ does not here predict a cataclysmic coming, then, words have no meaning (40,46). But some say that Jesus subscribed to Jewish eschatology, which we no longer hold. That view involves a very grave implication, if it is true. Those who believe *all* that Christ said about anything need pay no attention to these dicta of unbelief. Christ said that he would come again, personally, visibly, suddenly, *and he will*. It only remains for us to relate ourselves aright to the fact.

How we may do so is shown in three brief parables. The first relates to **the fact of his coming** (35-38); the second, **to the time of his coming** (39,40); and the third, **to the issues of his coming** (41-48); and in view of these things, in each we are exhorted to faithfulness and watchfulness.

As to the *fact*, Jesus says that he will return (36). As to the *time*, he says that no one knows the hour (40). As to the *issues*, he says that he will reward the faithful (44), and punish the unfaithful (46). He plainly teaches that we are responsible for our ignorance; that there is no such thing as complete moral ignorance; that it is possible for men to sin in spite of light; that our privileges are the measure of our responsibilities.

These are tremendous lessons. Now, let me ask you, if you had *known* that Christ would come tomorrow morning, would you have lived this last week as you have done? You do not know that he will *not* come tomorrow!

Thought: Help and happiness are hidden in hope.

Luke 12:49-59

Warning and rebuke

Do not fail to observe that before the cross, Jesus spoke of *his second advent* (35-48). This means that with utmost certainty he saw beyond the cross the consummation far down the ages, already nearly 2,000 years. Think about that because of its tremendous personal implications.

Warning (49-53). Having thus spoken, Jesus then turns to the matter of *his first coming*, his presence with the people then, and the consequences of it. Frequently did Christ say *why he had come*, and some of these utterances appear, but only appear, to contradict one another. Whatever is meant by *fire* in verse 49, the effect of it is clear (51-53). The conjunction here of the figures of *fire* and *water* should be marked (49,50).

By his *baptism* shall come the *burning*. The former was what his coming involved for himself; the latter, what it involved for the world. The baptism was the cross; the burning is the controversy which it has engendered. Let us understand by verses 51-53 that this was the *effect* rather than the *design* of Christ's coming.

The genuineness of Jesus is reflected in this whole passage. What adventurer would predict the apparent failure of his mission? Christ never led men to expect what could not be. He prepared his disciples for disappointment – *division*. Many families have broken up over Christ, but that is not his fault.

Rebuke (54-59). Turning to the *people*, Jesus tells them that their weather-wisdom is just worldly wisdom; that they studied the sky that they might protect themselves from the *storm* and the *simoom*; but that they were religion-foolish when it came to the understanding of John the Baptist and himself.

He urges them to come to terms with their creditor before the magistrate pronounces sentence (58,59). This is a call to repentance. There is hope while you are still *on the way*. When you reach the end of the journey it will be too late.

Thought: A wrong road never led to a right end.

Luke 13:1-17

Goodness and severity

Christ calls the people to repentance (1-9), twice plainly and then by a parable, following on what he had just said (12:58,59). This means, of course, that we all have that for which we should repent, and that repentance is *our* responsibility. Reference is made to two recent events of which there is no record anywhere else; of the fate that befell a number of people, (a) by the collision of Galileans with Romans, and (b) by the collapse of a Jerusalem tower (1-5). Christ does not say that these calamities were due to the sins of the victims, though the people thought that; but he does say that *unless sinners repent they shall perish*.

It is this solemn truth which the following parable enforces (6-9). The fig-tree is the Jewish nation and also, any individual soul. The point of the parable is damaged by the omission in the AV of *also* in verse 7. 'Why also cumbereth it the ground?' That is, not only is the tree barren, but it is also injuring the soil by robbing other plants of sap and sun. It is bad enough when a man does no good, but worse when he does positive harm.

God intends that you and I should be fruitful. Are we? Mercy is mingled with judgement. When the worst is known a margin time is allowed for repentance. Have you not had an extra year? And what have you done with it?

Christ heals a crippled woman (10-17). The following story is very graphic. Only Christ could *lift up* the soul that Satan had *bowed down* (11). And he not only *lifted* her, but also *loosed* her (12). It is wonderful to be lifted and loosed. The word *straight* is used of *setting up* the tabernacle (Acts 15:16). This architect of souls builds straight.

But, of course, somebody must grumble (14). If this man's religion could not save him from such an attitude, common humanity might have done so, and the Lord brings that home to him (15,16). The same work and word bring joy and shame (17). Meanness ought to be ashamed.

Thought: He hinders who will not help.

Luke 13:18-35

Kingdom truths

In verses 18-21, are **a pair of parables on the kingdom** of God. The view of the first, the *mustard seed*, is external; and of the second, the *leaven*, internal. Some take the first to mean that there would be an unnatural growth of the kingdom; and the second to mean that the kingdom would be corrupted. Others regard the first as telling that the kingdom would, at last, embrace all nations, and the second, as declaring that it would transform the whole of human life. Study these parables in their sermon-setting in Matthew 13.

Jesus was busy **on the way**, and all the way, to the cross (22). The answer he gave to any inquirer revealed that inquirer. Here he shows that the question in verse 23 was born of curiosity and not of concern.

The whole passage (23-30) is on **the danger of being excluded from the kingdom**. For *strait gate* read *narrow door*. In Matthew 7:13, it is *gate*, but not here. No one can slip through; everyone must *strive* (24). The kindred noun is used of Christ's *agony* in Gethsemane. The door will not be open for ever. Some will be shut out (25). *Contact* with Christ is not necessarily *connection* (26). Contemplate the sharply contrasted pictures in 27-29. The cry of verse 25, does not proceed from repentance, but from fear, and so these people never enter.

The mention of east, west, north and south (29) anticipates Revelation 7:9; the conversion of *Gentiles*, as verse 28, assumes the fate of unbelieving *Jews*.

Jesus' sorrow for Jerusalem (31-35). No doubt what the Pharisees reported of Herod's desire was correct (31), otherwise, Jesus would have replied to them, and not have sent a message to him (32). His life could not be cut short; he would fulfil his mission (32,33). Jerusalem well-nigh had a monopoly of martyrdoms: Jesus speaks ironically (33), and then, immediately, melts with tender grief over the degenerate city (34), the Temple of which is no longer God's, but their own (35).

Thought: God-opposition is self-destructing.

Luke 14:1-14

Feast lessons

● **Be merciful** (1-6). Of the seven miracles of mercy on the Sabbath, Luke records four (4:38; 6:6; 13:13; and here). What better day on which to do good? Yet, there were those who by their words and attitude made it an offence (1-6; 13:14). These showed compassion for asses and oxen but not for men and women (5; 13:15). How crooked the thinking of some people is! Some minds would be weightier if they threw overboard some of their cargo. It was abominably rude of this Pharisee to invite Jesus to be his guest, only that he might criticise what he did (1). And the rest of the company seem to have been rude also (7).

● **Be humble** (7-11). Against these, Jesus speaks a parable on *humility* (8-10). Verse 11 is the key. This is not a lesson on etiquette, but a declaration that humility is a condition of promotion in the kingdom of God. Surely nothing is more wonderful than Christ's creaturely humility (Philippians 2:5-8; John 13:4-17). Enough. Lie low. Willingness to be small is a sign of greatness. Only the really small ape greatness. Bumptious people are only baboons.

● **Be kind** (12-14). The whole passage, from verses 1 to 24, is about feasts. The previous discourse was addressed to the *guests* (7-11); this one (12-14) is addressed to the *host*. That was on humility; this is on kindness. Jesus does not teach that it is wrong for one to entertain friends and rich neighbours, but that we should not invite these *only*. It is good when we do good just for the sake of having done good.

The resurrection of the just is a germ idea, and implies a select resurrection distinct from a general resurrection. This is developed in the Epistles.

Mercy, humility and kindness are virtues not to be admired merely, but to be practised.

Thought: Table tactics tell a tale.

Luke 14:15-24

The great refusal

This parable of **the great Supper** and the parable of *the wedding garment* (Matthew 22:1-14) have much in common, but are not the same. This one follows from a remark dropped at the table (15). The things to mark here are, the prepared supper, the first invitations, the refusals, the second invitations, the third, and the full house.

Distinguish the *bidding* in verse 16, and the *reminding* in verse 17. If these persons had not wanted to go to the feast they should have said so when they were *bidden*. By not doing so they had virtually accepted the invitation, and now, when they are told that all is ready, they beg off.

Three refusals are recorded, and in each case, it is an *excuse* and not a *reason* that is offered. Never yet has anyone been able to show a *reason* for not accepting the gospel invitation. Furthermore, observe that these excuses related to things that were lawful and good. It is quite right to buy ground, and oxen, and to marry; but it is quite wrong to make any of these things a substitute for coming to Christ. Too often it is the good that keeps us from the best.

It is a terrible thing when love is *angry* (21)! I know of no more fearsome phrase than *the wrath of the Lamb*. Dread that! The first invitation was given to the Jews, but as they refused, it was then given to those whom the Jews despised (21), the publicans and sinners (Romans 11:25).

God's house shall be *filled* (23) though many shut themselves out. All the excluded are self-excluded, and all the included have accepted. Such refusal as these men were guilty of is still common, irrational, and fatal. It is amazing that any of us were ever invited to the feast. It is more amazing that anyone should refuse to go.

Thought: To flout the feast is fatal folly.

Luke 14:25-35

Conditions of discipleship

This great subject is unfolded here by way of *declaration, illustration, and application.* **The declaration (26,27).** Two conditions of discipleship are laid down; the soul must *forsake* (26), and *follow* (27), and forsake by following, for there is no true following of Christ where there is not the will and purpose, if need be, to forsake all else.

● **The illustration (28-32).** A double illustration is given of this: first, *the unfinished tower;* second, *the unwaged war.* These present the two aspects of a disciple's life — *within,* and *without; private* and *public; building* and *battling.*

A case is supposed. In the first parable, mark *the promising start, the tragical failure,* and *the withering scorn:* and in the second parable mark, *the spirited challenge, the sudden collapse,* and *the shameful compromise.*

A course is enjoined. First, think of the cost of building and battling, and then, say if you can even begin to build and battle. The Pharisee was confident that he could; the publican was sure that he could not.

A conclusion is implied. Man has no resources in himself for the work within, or for the war without. That is the first fact; and the second is, all necessary resources are in Christ, who is the master builder and the mighty conqueror, who said, 'I will build my church . . . the gates of hell shall not prevail.'

● **The application (33-35).** The *unalterable* condition of Christian discipleship, and the *universal* condition also, is that in all things, always, he be *first.* Christ has the right to ask and claim that of you and of me, and each of us is under the necessity of saying whether we will follow him or not. What answer have you given to him? What answer will you give him now?

Thought: Christlessness means collapse and defeat.

Luke 15:1-10

Sensibly and insensibly lost

This chapter is in Luke only, and it is, perhaps, the best known chapter in the Bible. Two things should be observed at once: first, the occasion of this utterance, which is the key to its interpretation; and second, that the three parables are really one, viewed from three standpoints.

The occasion tells of two classes of persons, *publicans and sinners*, on the one hand, *Pharisees and scribes* on the other hand; and both classes are to be found in each of the three parables. The former are represented by the one sheep, the one bit of silver, and the prodigal son; and the latter are represented by the ninety-nine sheep, the nine bits of silver, and the elder brother.

Publicans and Pharisees, sinners and scribes were all equally *lost*, but some were conscious of the fact, and admitted it, and the others were not, and did not. The whole chapter illustrates Jesus' sayings, 'I came not to call the *righteous*, but sinners to repentance;' and 'He that is *whole* hath no need of a physician, but he that is *sick*.'

The teaching. Christ does not teach that there are any who are *righteous* and *whole*, but that there are many who think they are, and he says that his salvation cannot reach them. Our fear and pity should be for the ninety-nine sheep, the nine coins and the elder son, for their insensibility of their condition is the worst feature of their lost state. There is some hope for those who know something of their need.

One other thing should be observed, considering the chapter as a whole: namely, that it displays the concern of the triune God for the salvation of sinners. The shepherd represents Christ; the woman represents the Spirit-indwelt Christian or church; and the father represents the Father. The three persons of the one Godhead long for your salvation and mine. The details of each parable should be carefully studied, but get this comprehensive view first of all.

Thought: There is blessing for the bleating.

Luke 15:11-32

Brothers apart

The two truths which this chapter so powerfully illustrates are, *man's sin* and *God's love*. Our sin is not determined by our sensibility of it, and God's love is not dependent upon our acknowledgement of it. All men sin, and God loves all men. Those are the two facts which make necessary and possible the gospel. The three things to mark in the prodigal's story are – *the going, the absence,* and *the return*.

Recently, I heard an outline on this, which, while it may cause a smile, nevertheless presents the essential facts of the case; and so I pass it on, not for your amusement, but instruction. ● **His badness.** Here we see him *cavilling, travelling* and *revelling.* ● **His sadness.** Here we learn that he *goes to the dogs, eats with the hogs,* and *home he jogs.* ● **His gladness.** Here he *received a seal, ate of the veal,* and *danced a reel.*

It is easy to wander; but how difficult to return! Satan is a hard master. Friends drawn by one's money last only while the money lasts. It was a most terrible humiliation for a Jew to have to feed pigs! But his destitution led to reflection, his reflection to repentance, and his repentance to resolve.

Notice the prayer he prepared, and how much of it he prayed when he got back (18,21). What a welcome the Father gives to every sinner who comes home! *He began to be in want*, but that beginning had an ending. Then, *he began to be merry*, and he is merry still (14,24).

What a contrast is the elder brother, the proud Pharisee. He was in his father's house, but not of it; in other words, he was a church member, but not a Christian. He was trusting to morality for salvation. He would not own his brother; *thy son* he contemptuously said (30). It is the story of 18:9-14, seen from the standpoint of the home, instead of the temple. Forgiveness is possible while time lasts.

Thought: Carnal pride and spiritual poverty go together.

Luke 16:1-18

What sinners can teach saints

This has been considered the most perplexing of all our Lord's parables. A servant robbed his master, and yet received his master's praise, and was pointed to by Jesus as an example for his followers. And further; it seems to teach that a place in heaven can be purchased with money. But what is here commended is not this steward's dishonesty, but his *foresight* and *prudence*. He is not praised for doing what was wrong, but for a sharpness and ingenuity which were worthy of a better occasion.

The key is verse 8b. We may learn much from worldlings. The sinners' realities are real to them. They believe in bed, board and a balance at the bank, and so believe in them that they live for them. Does the saint believe in the *eternal* as the sinner believes in the *temporal*? Saints may learn from sinners. This steward made provision for tomorrow. He had been entrusted with his master's interests, and would have to give account. He had been unfaithful, and made preparation for eventualities.

Have not we been entrusted by a greater master with greater interests? And shall not we have to give an account? And ought not we to prepare for a longer tomorrow? *Future spiritual blessing may be secured by a right use of present temporal advantages.*

There are small tests of great principles (10-12). It is our faithfulness in little things that reveals our character; and faithfulness is the child of loyalty (13). We all are in danger of the divided heart, of trying to reconcile incompatibles of compromise. But it is a universal and unalterable fact that *no man can serve two masters.*

Verses 14-17 teach that God is the searcher of our hearts. Traditionalism is not always the friend of truth.

Thought: Believe aright, and live for what you believe.

Luke 16:19-31

Character and destiny

The previous lesson was about the steward of a rich man: this lesson is about a rich man himself. That lesson was not without its difficulties, neither is this one. Neither of these stories is called a *parable*, and there are reasons for thinking that the one now before us is not a parable; for example, the mention of two persons, *Lazarus* and *Abraham*. That the story is clothed in figurative language (23) is evident, but behind and beneath are the most solemn realities.

Our Lord is not teaching that it is a vice to be rich, or a virtue to be poor. He is not teaching that the rich go to hell, and the poor go to heaven. But he is teaching that *a man's use of his advantages is a revelation of his character*, and that *character determines destiny*.

Here are two strongly contrasted pictures. **Two men in this life** (19-21). Rich and poor; manor and street; satisfied and hungry; robes and rags; well and ill. So they lived their earthly life. They were fellow-men, and neighbours, and each, in his own way, was related to the other. That is true of us all. **Two men in the next life** (22-31). What a contrast! Angels carried Lazarus' soul to the glory; men carried Dives' body to the grave. The one experienced rapture, and the other remorse. The tables were reversed, not because the one was poor, but because he was good; and not because the other was rich, but because he was bad.

This story does not teach that if we do good in this world we shall go to heaven, for salvation is not by works; but it does teach that *lovelessness is an indication of spiritual death*, and that brings its own penalty. Destiny is determined *in this life*; in the other world, character is fixed (26). The rich man implies that he had not been given a fair chance (27,28). But if men will not heed the testimony of the living, neither would they the witness of the dead. This rich man began to *pray* too late (27). Be warned!

Thought: Memory will bring bliss or burning.

Luke 17:1-10

Christian ethics

How much Christ said in a few words on big subjects! His teaching was not systematic, but is easily systematised. Collect, classify, and correlate all that he said, for instance on the *Father*, the *Holy Spirit*, *himself*, on *sin, repentance, forgiveness* and *prayer*.

Here he speaks on **stumbling blocks** (1,2). These, he says, are inevitable in such a world as this, but that inevitability does not absolve anyone of his responsibility for occasioning them. The individual's sin always goes beyond himself, and he is responsible for the damage it does to others, especially to those who are young or weak in the faith. It is better that one should be out of this world — better for others, that is — than that he should stay here to hinder others.

The next lesson is on **forgiveness** (3,4). The preceding passage speaks of *giving* offence, this one of *taking* offence. Here we are taught that a *brother* can injure us; that we should *rebuke* such a one; that every such offender should *repent*; that when the one repents the other should *forgive*; and that we should not put a limit on forgiveness so long as there is repentance. We should distinguish between the *spirit* of forgiveness, and the *act*. The latter is conditioned on repentance; the former is not.

The surprise and exclamation of the disciples (5) leads to the next lesson, on **faith** (5-10). Much faith would be needed for so much forgiveness, but faith is a mighty power; it can do things which are humanly impossible (6). What follows is connected in this way: 'When you exercise such faith do not become selfish and haughty, as you would incline to be, but remember that when you have done your utmost you are only a servant, and have only done your *duty*' (7-10). This is a too little known and too little understood parable. Service widely differs — some *plough*, and some *feed cattle*, and some do other things — but in all, the servant is subject to his Lord.

Thought: Proud faith is a spiritual monstrosity.

Luke 17:11-25

Negligence

The ten lepers (11-19). This is a solemn lesson on **ingratitude**. But for Jesus, their condition was hopeless; they were all perfectly healed of the most loathsome disease, and yet, nine of the ten did not trouble themselves to return and say, 'Thank you,' to their benefactor. The one who did was the only one who might have been excused had he not done so, for he was a Samaritan, a *stranger* (16,18).

Many cry to God when they are in distress, who forget him when they are delivered. If sickness moves us to prayer, health should move us to praise. These men were not without faith, for when they left Jesus they were still leprous. They were told to report their healing to the priest, while still they were in the grip of the disease; and it was only on the way that they were delivered. Such faith should have been less forgetful. The nine went to some Jewish priest. Was he at all responsible for their default? The one who started out to find a Samaritan priest, apparently never went; as soon as he was healed he returned.

Jesus' omniscience is seen in that he knew all ten were healed on the way. A second blessing awaited the one who returned (19). God has always more to give to the grateful.

The coming of the kingdom (20-37). The Pharisees were looking into the *future*, but Jesus calls their attention to the *present* (20-21). The kingdom, he says, is seen by the soul, not by the senses. For *within you* read *is in your midst*. What they were looking for was there, but they were too blind to see it.

Verses 22-25 describe how and when Jesus will reappear on the earth. This universal coming (24) should be distinguished from the later revelation of 1 Thessalonians 4:13-18. The glorious future was ever in Christ's view, but so was also the cross, as the way to it (25). Every holy hope is in danger of being deceived (23). Pray for spiritual sanity.

Thought: Take the trouble to say 'thanks'.

Luke 17:26-37

Coming judgement

In pursuance of the subject of his coming again, Christ says that *history repeats itself. As . . . so.* Men profit from previous experience in nothing less than in spiritual things. Carnal security long ago was overtaken by judgement. Jesus says that this will happen again, yet how few believe him. The things which those people of old did (27,28), were not wrong, but that they lived for those things, and in them, and regarded neither God nor their own souls, were wrong. Carnalism, temporalism, materialism, mammonism, as principles, are always wrong, and these things rule today as they did in that far off day. But God's moral government of the world is just, and so there must be judgement, and man's disbelief cannot delay it.

We are told, furthermore, that that *judgement shall be discriminating*; it will be a day of separations (34-36). Some will be taken, and others left. This is interpreted by some as meaning, 'taken for judgement, and left for blessing'; and by others as meaning, 'taken for blessing and left for judgement'. Regarding all the teaching of the New Testament on the subject, the latter will be true of the first stage of the advent, and the former true of the second stage.

But what makes the difference? The answer is in verse 33. Here is a solemn warning: those referred to in 26-29 were altogether careless, but Lot's wife (32) had made the first step towards escaping the future destruction. She started, and then stuck. Her husband was left for blessing, but she was taken for judgement. They who start must strive if they would arrive.

Body in verse 37 refers to that which is ripe for judgement, and the *eagles* tell of instruments of judgement. It is upon the carcasses that the birds come: judgement is never before its time. What Christ says about the future is not his *opinion*, it is *revelation*, and must come to pass.

Thought: Live the present in the light of the future.

Luke 18:1-17

How to pray

Here are two parables on **prayer**. The one is a lesson on *persistence*, and the other on *reality*. The scene of the one is the *court*, and of the other, the *Temple*. In the one are a man and a woman, and in the other two men. In the one, only one prays, and in the other, both pray.

The first is generally called the parable of *the unjust judge* but it were better called that of **the persistent widow** (1-8), for Jesus says that the lesson is, we '*must always pray and never lose heart*' (1).

Sharply contrasted are this judge's unwillingness to answer the woman, and God's willingness to answer us; and by implication, her persistence where there was unwillingness, and our scepticism where there is willingness. The judge said, in effect, '*Because she annoys me I will give her justice to prevent her from constantly coming to pester me*'; but God says that he will answer '*infinitely beyond all our highest prayers or thoughts*' (Ephesians 3:20). Delay is not denial (7), and so, delay should not discourage. *Never lose heart* (1).

The second is the parable of **the Pharisee and the tax-gatherer** (9-14). The latter is one of three who figure in the gospels: cf. Levi, and Zacchaeus. All three got converted. Now, both these men went to the temple to *pray*; one did pray, and the other did not.

Prayer is not what comes out of our mouth, but out of our heart. Jesus says, that the Pharisee *stood erect* (11), but that the collector *stood far back* (13). Here attitudes are symptoms. The Pharisee's face was so swollen with pride that his eyes could not see God. Study these two prayers (11-13), and then, pray to please God (14).

An incomparable incident on **Jesus in relation to children** is given in verses 15-17. I should imagine the disciples had no children of their own.

Thought: Broken hearts are better than bumptious arts.

Luke 18:18-30

A poor rich man

This story of **the rich young man** left a deep impression on the disciples for it is recorded by three of the evangelists. We assume that his inquiry was in all seriousness and we see that it was supreme. *Eternal life* is vastly more than endless life: the expression always points to *the quality of the life*. The sinlessnesss of Jesus is in no wise endangered by his reply in verse 19; on the contrary, the strangeness of it might well have called attention to the deeper truth. Jesus was declining the epithet from this young man because he was not giving to it a deep enough content.

Being thrown back upon the law, the ruler claims to have carefully obeyed it always. Jesus neither assents nor dissents to this claim; but seeing that the man prides himself on *doing*, he will give him something more to do (22). Be careful to understand that this is not a rule for all men, but *a test for one man*. Jesus knew that the youth's money came between him and full surrender of himself to God. Whatever does that, must be got rid of. Christ never spoke against riches as such.

This youth possessed much, but the *one lack* rendered all the rest of no avail for the purpose. He was like a costly watch without a mainspring; like a luxurious automobile without an engine: only one thing lacking, but that was the one thing that mattered. His money, which was a trust, became a temptation; all our trusts may become that, and do, if they are given a wrong place in our life.

Jesus' reply to the ruler which led the hearers to despair of salvation (26), led Peter to hope for extraordinary reward (28). Mark the answer given to the apostles (29,30). Material reward is not promised for material sacrifice, but for the latter there will be spiritual reward, and not only in the life to come. *Many times as much* shows that we are all always hopelessly in God's debt. We cannot say whether this young ruler ever got what he lacked, but his case is a solemn warning to us.

Thought: There will be no pockets in your shroud.

Luke 18:31-43

The blind beggar blessed

The third prediction of his passion (31-34). For the third time Jesus plainly tells his disciples of his coming *passion*. Take time to be impressed by this, because it is proof alike of his humanity and divinity; of his humanity, for he was soon to die; and of his divinity for he would rise again three days later. His supernatural knowledge is shown by the details into which he goes, and his divine self-consciousness is shown by what he says of himself in verse 31. But the disciples were bewildered (34). Pascal has said, 'one must know human things in order to love them, but one must love divine things if he would rightly know them.'

The blind beggar (35-43). This is a familiar story. The man is face to face with the three powers of life – *self, the world*, and *God*. In the first, is *need*, in the third, *supply*, and in the second, *hindrance*. Deliverance is better than dole. The world gave this man the latter, but Jesus gave him the former.

All here is very swift and definite. Jesus was *passing by*; he soon would be past; it must be now or never for the blind man. His cries were short. Jesus' inquiry was short, the man's reply was short. There is the sense of earnestness and urgency about it all.

A man facing his one great opportunity in life has neither time nor use for verbiage. The cry of sinners is not adorned with flowers of speech, but rises nakedly and piercingly from broken hearts.

If Christ stood before you just now and asked, '*What shall I do for you?*' what answer would you give him? He appeals, not to our *wants*, but to our *needs*. A condemned murderer does not want flowers, but a reprieve; a drowning man does not want sympathy, but a deliverer; whatever sinners *want*, they urgently and supremely *need* God's forgiveness and a new life. *Faith* is the link between our need and the divine supply (42). Then – *believe to see*.

Thought: Let no one stand between you and Christ.

Luke 19:1-10

Up a tree

Levi, and the man who went to the temple, were both tax-collectors, but Zacchaeus was a *chief* among such. He had grown wealthy, but not happy, by extortion. By the way in which he had lined his pocket he had improverished his soul. Well, he had heard of Jesus, and his curiosity was aroused; but we must believe that beneath his curiosity was a measure of concern, for he knew that all was not well with him. If he had any pride, he certainly overcame it when he climbed up into the sycamore tree. Perhaps he thought that he could see without being seen there, but foliage was no cover from Jesus' flashing eyes.

How often a crowd prevents a man from seeing Jesus! Why not get alone somewhere, and see him? He sees all who are looking for him. Never before were so many eyes at once fixed upon this little man, and never before had he been addressed in this way (5). He must have almost fallen from the branch with wonder.

Jesus' friendliness was all the more wonderful to him because he had forfeited the friendship of everyone else. The most hardened hearts respond to kindness. But listen to this surly crowd. '*They all began muttering with indignation.*' Of course they did not know that the guest of sinners becomes the host of saints, but he does. Jesus knew that this fruit was ready to pluck. What a conversion! Heaven's light flashed full into the darkness of his heart and chased it all away.

What was graciously done was ethically proved. It was not a case of making a new start only, the new thing that had come into his life went into the past to straighten things out. How had he amassed all that money? He'll now endeavour to place it where it belonged (8). He was not saved because he did that: he did that because he was saved. Verse 10 is one of the greatest utterances in all the Bible.

Thought: If you will come down, Jesus will come in.

Luke 19:11-27

A pound apiece

Undoubtedly this parable has an historical basis. On the death of Herod the Great, Archelaus went to Rome to obtain the emperor's confirmation of his father's will and the kingdom of Judah. An embassy was sent after him to protest against his reigning over Judah (14). However, Archelaus was appointed. During his absence he had left his money affairs in charge of servants (13). When he returned to Palestine, he slew all his opponents (27), and rewarded his supporters (17).

All this is made to represent a great programme in human history: the *departure* of Christ in AD 30; his long *absence*, already nearly 2,000 years; and his *return* at the end of the age. He, too, during his absence, has committed a trust to his servants, and when he comes back he will call them to account. Several great lessons stand out in this parable.

● **The declaration that Christ is to come back** (12,13,15). By no process of interpretation can this be made to mean a continuous spiritual coming. The return will be as definite as the departure.

● **The intimation that he will be away for an indefinite period** (12). The teaching of Jesus did not warrant the expectation of a speedy return; indeed, in Matthew 25:19, it says that his absence would last *a long time*.

● **During his absence his servants are not only to watch but also to work** (13). Each of us is given the same capital with which to work. Surely the *pound* represents *eternal life*. This is where the parable differs from that of Matthew 25:14-30. There, unequal ability means varying opportunity; but here, equal grace means equal responsibility.

● **The life of each of us will be called to account** (15). Wherever there is opportunity, there is responsibility. The facts of man and God mean that man is accountable to God.

● **Rewards will be according to one's faithfulness, or unfaithfulness** (17,19,24).

Thought: We are responsible for the use we make of ourselves.

Luke 19:28-40

Palm Sunday

With this portion begins what is called **the Passion Week**, and this event took place on what, in the Christian calendar, is called **Palm Sunday**. Remember, the Jewish day ran from sunset to sunset.

Without doubt Jesus here accepts messianic honours, in fulfilment of Zechariah 9. What would have happened if all Jerusalem had acknowledged his claim, and crowned him king? Would we ever have had the New Testament? That is speculative, but what is clear is that God's purpose and man's free will are both factors in human history.

One cannot fail to observe in this account with what care for detail Christ entered upon the solemn events of this momentous week. He chose an *ass* on which to enter Jerusalem. He was the King of Peace. The *horse* in Scripture is generally the warhorse (Zechariah 10:3). The record gives no evidence of a previous arrangement, yet the owner of this ass responded at once (31). Surely he who was *the Lord* (31) knew just what would happen!

The whole procedure here is unlike the whole previous action of Jesus, who had refused the honours of the people. Do not overlook the phrase, *the whole multitude of the disciples*. Christ, even at this time, had innumerable followers (cf. 1 Corinthians 15:6); he had made a tremendous impression upon the people in these three years. Herein is a mighty conjunction – the city, the Temple, the people, and the king – but the conjunction proved a conflict and not a consummation. Then, was the divine purpose thwarted by men? Oh no. God can afford to wait.

Many assume that the messianic kingdom was never intended to be visible, and that Christ's kingship is now being fulfilled in the hearts of believers, but the Old Testament and the Gospels do not lend themselves to that view, and the events of Palm Sunday are against it. But Christ should be Lord in your life.

Thought: It is easier to shout than to surrender.

Luke 19:41-48

Sad sights

Weeping over Jerusalem (41-44). The account of *Sunday* continues to the end of verse 44. The disciples' joy was met by the Master's sorrow; their laughter, by his tears. He *beheld the city* (41). Of what memories was it the embodiment! From the day when David conquered the Jebusites until this entry hour, this city had played a notable part in the history of the world, and had probably suffered more than any other city.

He who 'beheld it' knew all its past, present and future; all three are in verses 42,43. Here is a prediction of the calamitous overthrow of Jerusalem, which took place forty years later, when Titus led the Roman hosts against it. That event, from which the Jews have not yet recovered, overtook them because *they knew not the time of their visitation* (44). When they could, they would not, and so when they would, they could not. That is a law which operates all the time. *Time* implies limitation; the day of opportunity comes to an end. He who is sleepy at sunrise, and lazy at mid-day, shall suffer at sundown.

The cleansing of the Temple (45,46). This took place on Monday, Nisan 11th. Jesus opened and ended his ministry in this way (cf. John 2:12-16). Mark carefully his two Old Testament quotations, Isaiah 56:7 and Jeremiah 7:11.

Teaching at the Temple (47,48). What follows summarises his programme during this eventful week. How courageous he is, and yet, how cautious! What energy he displays in sight of the end!

On the other hand, his enemies are at once indignant and impotent (48). *The people all hung upon his lips*, as a young bird upon the mother feeding it. But that is not enough for him who *hung upon the cross* for us. Hanging interest is compatible with hugging sin. Let us heed what we hear.

Thought: He who opposes God ruins himself.

Luke 20:1-18

Battle at close quarters

The next two chapters relate the doings and sayings of Jesus on the *Tuesday* of Passion Week. The two parts of our portion, verses 1-8 and 9-18, are closely related, the latter being a photograph of the former.

The authority of Jesus questioned (1-8). Jesus was busy to the end. He did not allow his approaching suffering to cut short his energetic serving. In the shadow of the cross he *preached the gospel*, which that cross alone made possible (1).

The parties named in verse 1, were the three classes who composed the *Sanhedrin*. The implication of their questions was that Jesus was an unlicensed teacher; that he had not been properly ordained. They made the mistake then, which is being made still, of supposing that the validity of spiritual ministry consisted in some form of ordination, and the sanction of some body of persons. The man whom God calls to preach needs no such recognition.

Those who here claimed to have authority to question another's authority were singularly lacking in straightforwardness: *If we say . . . he will say . . . but and if we say . . . they will stone us*. They were guilty of either inconsistency or cowardice, and probably of both; yet, in their view, they were the people to authorise others to preach and teach!

The parable of the tenants (9-16). What Jesus thought of them is seen in the parable which follows. The *certain man* represents God; the *vineyard*, the Jewish people; the *husbandmen*, their leaders; the *servants*, the prophets; and the *son*, Christ himself. This is just history in parable form.

The parable of the stone (17,18). The fate of the evil-doers is told, and by another parable other issues are foretold. The *husbandmen* are now the *builders*, and the *son* is now the *stone*. The despised one would ultimately dominate, Jesus says. This was predicted long before. See Psalm 118:22: cf. Isaiah 8:14,15; Daniel 2:44. In effect, Jesus' amazing declaration is, that he who is shortly to be killed, will afterwards be crowned.

Thought: Conviction too often falls short of conversion.

Luke 20:19-36

Talk traps

In nothing can one be so easily trapped as in his talk. The tongue is the cause of endless trouble. But the tongue is only a servant: its master is behind. Here are men who were not honest, but who were to act the part (20); that is, they were professional humbugs. But their treacherous fingers could not get hold of Jesus' honest speech (20,26). They endeavoured to get him into *political* trouble by forcing him to take the side of the Jews, or of the Romans (20-26). There did not seem to be any way out. But Jesus showed, what is so often the case, that the truth does not lie in one or other of two views, but in them both.

Every Christian bears a relation to both the church and the state. To deny the latter relation and obligation is just nonsense. The fact that 'our citizenship is in heaven' does not affect this other fact, that we pay for a police force, and are glad of its protection. Verse 25 should straighten out the thinking of a lot of people.

The next attack was from a *doctrinal* angle (27-36), and came from people who had no belief in spiritual realities. Their creed consisted mainly in denials. It's a pity when a man parades his ignorance. Some people might be thought wise if only they would keep their mouths shut.

The only value which attaches to the shallow superciliousness of these Sadducees is in that it drew from Jesus so profound a pronouncement on things which lie in the future. He reveals that 'children of God' shall rise from the dead; that in the life beyond, sex considerations will not exist; that there will be no need for them, as no one will ever die. These are not speculations, but revelations. Christ said not a little about the future which awaits us all. Let us heed what he said both for encouragement and warning.

Thought: Feigned superiority is unfeigned stupidity.

Luke 20:37-47

A poser

The scribes who compliment Jesus (39), *he condemns* (46). Flattery is one of the subtlest snares, and very few can courteously resist it. They may easily fall to praise who would rigorously withstand persecution. Jesus ever remained untouched by anything but the truth.

Well, so far others have attacked and he has defended, but now *he attacks and they find themselves unable to defend* (41-44).

This is a famous passage for many reasons. The chief of these is that here *Jesus plainly claims for himself divinity*. Psalm 110 was an acknowledged messianic Psalm: it taught that Messiah would be divine; Jesus, by his words and deeds claimed to be Messiah; therefore he was divine. Read the full text in Matthew 22:41-46.

Three persons are introduced in the Psalm: *Jehovah*, *Adonai*, and *David*. It was Jehovah who said to David's Adonai, 'Sit Thou . . .'; yet this Adonai is called David's son. How? Read Isaiah 9:6,7. He who was the *offspring* was also the *root* of David (Revelation 22:16); he who came from him was before him: that is, this man was God.

Of course these scribes could not answer this question; their theology stood in the way of truth. Theology has done that widely.

Incidentally, Christ says that David wrote the 110th Psalm. Present day criticism is practically unanimous in saying that he did not write it. Who should know?

When Christ portrayed a character or a class, he did it with absolute accuracy; then, who could hold a brief for the scribes after reading verses 46,47? Three words sum them up – *vanity*, *avarice* and *hypocrisy*. The ideas attached to *humility*, *compassion* and *genuineness* were foreign to them. All such are people to *beware of*.

Thought: Truth is a burning as well as a shining light.

Luke 21:1-13

Forecasts

What is the real worth of a human action? That depends partly on the nature of the action, but chiefly on the motive of it. The intrinsic value of two mites was practically nil, yet Jesus said that this widow, putting that into the treasury, had put in more than all the other gifts together. What was the standard of judgement? This — that love is measured by sacrifice. The *all* of penury was vastly more than the *some* of plenty. It is the heart that determines the value of any gift.

If in the first paragraph (1-4) Jesus regarded *little as much*, in the second (5,6), he regards *much as little*. The two mites were cherished, but the goodly stones are to be cast down. No material splendour in a religious building is of any real value, if the place is not serving a spiritual end. For this lack the Temple was doomed.

The disciples ask two questions: *what?* and *when?*, and these are answered in the discourse which follows (8-36). Two things should be carefully distinguished in this discourse; the *fall of Jerusalem*, and the *second advent of Christ*. The latter is predicted in verses 8-11, 25-36; and the former, in verses 12-24. Mark the words, *before all these* (12), and the fate of Jerusalem *until the times of the Gentiles be fulfilled* (24).

In forecasting the future, Jesus did not paint a golden age, a rising race, a world 'fit for heroes to live in'. No, he talked about deceivers, wars, earthquakes, famines, pestilences, fearful sights, persecutions, prisons; and although these things are not all, yet, the fact of these things at all shows that the world is wildly astray from God, and proves the necessity for Christ's return. Prophecy is the mould of history, and history is the authentication of prophecy. Christ's forecasts are not false.

Thought: Infidelity renders nothing that is true invalid.

Luke 21:14-24

AD 70

We have said that two things must be distinguished in verses 8-36: *the prophecy of Christ's second advent* (8-11, 25-36); and *the prophecy of the destruction of Jerusalem* (12-24). You will observe that the nearer prediction is enclosed in the farther; and that though the farther has not yet been fulfilled, the nearer was fulfilled in AD 70. The words *before all these*, and *until the times* (12-24) are the distinguishing lines.

Fulfilment of verse 12 is recorded in the *Acts*. Christians appeared before Gallio, Felix, Festus, Agrippa, and Nero. The persecutions of Nero were a war against a name, but *in the end all this was evidence of their fidelity*, their sufferings helping forward the success of the church, and proving the guilt of their persecutors.

In verses 12-19, *the case of the Christians* is in view, but in 20-24, *the case of Jerusalem*, which was the embodiment of the nation. Look carefully at these two paragraphs, and observe that while encouragement is given in the first, only counsel is given in the second. The reason for this is, that the Christians were innocent, but the city was guilty: the former suffered for their fidelity, but the latter for their infidelity.

A Christian who is everywhere praised can hardly be faithful (17). Verse 18 cannot, in view of verse 16, be taken literally as it stands. The meaning must be that they were secure until God allowed them to be touched. We know that hair and head perished, but *they* did not, for *by their endurance they won their souls* (19).

The Roman army invaded the city, led by Titus (20). They who had lacked faith had to flee (21). Josephus tells the tragic story of Jerusalem's siege and fall.

Thought: Sin and punishment are inseparable.

Luke 21:25-38

Prophetic signs

Premonitions of Christ's second advent are given in verses 25-33, first by declaration (25-28); and then, by illustration (29,30), with affirmation (31-33). Some interpret verse 25 literally; and others regard it as figurative of governments and authorities. What is clear is, that the Lord's return is to be heralded by world unrest, by universal commotion. Such a time is *ours*, and present-day conditions *may* be these signs, though no one can say for certain that they *are*. Sometime or another the Son of man will come, and so we cannot afford to neglect any such evidences as are here set forth.

The children of God have nothing to fear from the prospect of Christ's return. On the contrary, when the signs of the advent appear we should *look up* and *lift up our heads*. Delight, not depression, becomes all who love the Lord and his appearing (28). Do all Christians believe that their Lord will come again? And of those who do, how many look forward with joy to the event?

Verse 32 has a double meaning, because in this discourse is a double prophecy. Relative to the *Jerusalem prophecy* (12-24), it means that some then living would see that event, which was but forty years distant, about a *generation*. And relative to the *advent prophecy*, it means the generation *of* which, rather than the one *to* which he speaks. Christ's *'verily'* can leave no reasonable person in any doubt.

Well, *such a prospect should influence conduct* (34-36), negatively (34), and positively, (36). Of course the past affects the present, but so should the future. Hope looking on should be as powerful as faith looking back. Here ends *Tuesday's* ministry, after which Jesus did not again enter the Temple as a teacher.

Verses 37,38, tell of how he spent the first three days of Passion Week. What a record!

Thought: Belief that does not affect behaviour is bosh.

Luke 22:1-13

A cursed contract

According to all the leading outlines of the Passion Week, the Wednesday is regarded as a day of retirement, of which we have no record. This is on the assumption that the crucifixion took place on the Friday, called Good Friday in the church's calendar. Both these views are open to challenge and Thursday may well have been the day of the crucifixion, in which case the problem of the *three days and three nights* in the tomb would be solved. But in the accepted view, verses 1-6 of this chapter belong to the *Wednesday*.

It is **Judas' day** (1-6), not Jesus'. How base human nature can be, even where there is a parade of piety. Here the veil is drawn aside, and we are shown the very emotions of these priests and scribes, first *fear*, and then *joy* (2,5). Their fear of the people prevented them doing straightway what they wanted to do, and so they resorted to *scheming*, and were *glad* when they saw some hope of succeeding.

Poor Judas! Can anything be said in extenuation of his conduct? I know of nothing. He sold eternal love for the price of a slave gored by an ox: an astoundingly bad bargain, if in our mind we can separate the ideas of deed and crime.

But Jesus went on with his work (7,8), by making **preparations for the Passover** (7-13). Hell could do nothing until heaven's hour had come. Seeing that so much is said about the place where Jesus and his disciples were to observe the Passover (9-13), it is strange that *the good man of the house* is not named. Was he Nicodemus, or Mark, or Joseph of Arimathea? He was a person of some wealth, and a disciple. Perhaps names were suppressed in those treacherous days out of consideration for the followers of Jesus. But the Master knew, and knows where all his disciples are, and he not only visits, but dwells in their homes. Blessed homes!

Thought: We can give to Christ only what belongs to him.

Luke 22:14-23

Two feasts

By a comparison of the four evangelical records, it becomes clear that Jesus and his disciples did not observe the Passover at the time which the Jews did, who were gathered in Jerusalem, but twenty-four hours earlier. Jesus' trial was over before the people observed the feast (John 18:28; 19:14), and Jesus' observance of it preceded his trial (John 13). That is the first important thing to observe.

And the second is that *two feasts* united in this celebration. In that 'upper room' a momentous event took place; the **Passover feast** was solemnly put to an end (16-18), and the **Lord's Supper** was as solemnly instituted (19,20). On that table one age ended, and another began; and Christ himself was the fulfilment of the one ordinance, and the fullness of the other.

John does not allude to the institution of the Lord's Supper, which, when he wrote his Gospel, was an established ordinance of the church; but he does record Jesus' teaching on the subject (chapter 6:32-58). What is said in verses 16,18, is generally taken to refer to a mystical celebration in heaven; but while not excluding that idea, surely there was an earlier fulfilment of the promise! Is not Jesus here referring to the supper about to be instituted (19,20), and did he not partake of that, with his disciples, some days later (24:30)?

Long and bitter controversy has raged round the Lord's Supper, and still does, for it is the most crucial question in Christendom today; but let us get back to its first simplicity: a perfect symbol of the greatest event in human history; the body and the bread, the blood and the wine, the disciples and all Christians. Nothing here of priestly pretensions, nor of materialistic virtue. Back to the beginning!

Thought: The Lord's table is his people's.

Luke 22:24-38

Rebuke, condemnation and warning

Verses 24-30, are peculiar to Luke, and are to be connected with the 'feet washing' recorded in John 13:4-17; probably following that event. How amazing that these men, after all that they had seen and heard, were in the shadow of the cross, **striving about supremacy** (24-27)!

But let us examine ourselves. Are not Christians still scrambling for seats? And do Christian ministers not nowadays angle for place and power? Do we not covet earthly honours, and often compromise to get them? Protestants may look down on the old monastic orders, but Augustine and his followers were not in pursuit of ecclesiastical preferments or worldly ease. The teaching of Christ is that he who rules may be contemptibly small, but that he who serves is in the way of greatness (25-27).

From rebuke Jesus swiftly turns to **commendation and promises** (28-30). He promises to his disciples honours which the ambitions of the flesh can never secure (29,30). It would appear that verse 29 refers to this life and world, and verse 30 to the next.

Now follows a brief and solemn conversation between **Jesus and Peter** (31-34). Observe that Satan's desire was to have all the apostles, *you* (plural); and that Christ's prayer was for Peter only, *thee* (singular).

Hath desired, means *to demand for oneself*, and *have prayed* means *have besought*. Jesus did not pray that Peter might not fall, which he did, but that his faith might not collapse, and it did not. Many Christians need to be *converted* (32). Peter was already regenerated. After this event can any of us be self-confident?

Christ, more concerned about his disciples' **future trials** (35-38) than about his fast approaching sufferings, tells them that the comparative severity of the past two and a half years will soon give place to opposition and persecution, for which they must be prepared. The language here is figurative.

Thought: The cock's crow convicted the cocksure.

Luke 22:39-53

The betrayal

Jesus prays on the Mount of Olives (39-46). According to the accepted chronology we have now reached the *Friday* of the Passover Week. This began at sunset on the Thursday, and it was late that night that Jesus left the upper room, and with his disciples crossed the Kidron, going to a garden with which he was familiar, here called *the place* (40). Eight of the disciples he left near the entrance and three of them went further in with him (Matthew 26:36,37).

An hour or two may have been spent here (39-46). Think on how it was spent. The darkness of the olive trees still hides from us much of this mystery, but we are allowed just a glimpse into it. If our eyes are not too tired, we may see that holy form upon the ground, and if our ears are not too heavy, we may hear his poignant prayer. Just for a moment the darkness is lit up by the flashing of an angel's wings (43).

The blood-shedding did not begin in the garden, but such was Jesus' agony that his sweat fell like clots of blood (44). Meanwhile, the disciples slept. They had had a trying time, and worse awaited them, and Christ did not blame them. His physical weakness was shown in sweat, and theirs in sleep; but it was costly sleep.

Jesus is arrested (47-53). And now, very early on Friday morning, perhaps nearer midnight, a crowd, led by Judas, came to arrest Jesus (47-53). It is a terrible story, but, as Jesus said to them, *'This is your hour.'* His great hour was yet to come, when, emerging from the grave, he would have forever conquered both death and it. Judas betrayed his Master with a kiss.

We know of only one other person who kissed him; the one was a kiss of hate, the other of love. By kissing Jesus, Judas cursed himself. Even in this dread hour, healing mercy was shown by Christ (51). Nothing could or can quench his love for sinners. And yet we sin! What a farce this armed crowd was! All the wolves of the forest came out against this one Lamb!

Thought: The sinless Sufferer is the sinner's Saviour.

Luke 22:54-71

Pretentious folly

The so-called *trial of Jesus* was in six stages; three were ecclesiastical, or Jewish, and three were civil, or Gentile. All this took place between 1 a.m. and 7 a.m. on Friday morning. The Jewish trials were all illegal, and the Gentile trials were all illogical, and all six were infamous. The first of the Jewish trials is recorded only by John (18:12-14, 19-23); the second and third are recorded by all four evangelists; here, before Caiaphas in verses 54, 63-65; and before the Sanhedrin in verses 66-71.

With the Jewish trials are associated two matters, *the denial of Peter*, and *the suicide of Judas*. The former (54-62) makes sad reading. Thrice he denied, and thrice he confessed (John 21). His loud confidence (33) swiftly gave way to base cowardice. He who said he would, didn't, and he who said he could, couldn't.

Do you say that you would not have acted like that if you had been there? You are only saying what Peter said before he fell. Christians should fear three foes – the flesh, the world, and the devil. David fell to the first, Demas, to the second, and Peter, to the third. We know that David and Peter tearfully repented. Peter and Judas both repented, but the latter too late. The early crowing of the cock should be a daily call to repentance.

The brutal conduct of the Jews (63-65) we cannot speak about: it is more execrable than that of the Romans.

Christ's claim for himself before the Sanhedrin is momentous (69,70). But these religionists, in their professed pursuit of the truth, persecuted it. No blindness is so complete as spiritual blindness, and no hearts can be so hard as those of religious sinners. These trials of Jesus are the darkest deeds in Jewish history. So long as the Jewish people endorse the verdict of nearly 2,000 years ago, so long will they suffer.

Thought: Better die than deny Christ.

Luke 23:1-12

The Roman trials

It is now Friday morning, and the *civil or Roman trials of Jesus* begin. The first was before Pilate, round about 5 a.m. (1-7); the second was before Herod, about 5.30 a.m. (5-12); and the third was before Pilate again, about 6.30 a.m. (13-25).

The first trial before Pilate (1-7). In this trial, the people addressed Pilate (2), Pilate questioned Jesus (3a), Jesus answered Pilate (3b), Pilate spoke to the people and their leaders (4), and these replied to Pilate (5). All this happened very quickly.

Three charges were brought by the Jews against Jesus. First, that he had upset and corrupted the nation; second that he refused to pay the Roman tax; and third that he claimed to be a king (2). Pilate showed his discernment by fixing on the last of these because it embraced the other two (3a). Jesus acknowledged that he was a king; John gives the conversation in detail (18:33-38). It was this detailed reply that led Pilate to the conclusion recorded in verse 4.

Maddened by this reply, the throng roared out their charge of sedition, indicating the scope of it (5). Again Pilate's astuteness comes into evidence by his fixing on the word *Galilee* (6), seeing in this a likely way of escaping his responsibility (7).

The trial before Herod (8-12). And so the second part of the farcical trial begins. Herod was the meanest mortal that ever wore a crown, a criminal and a clown. What can be said of the mentality of a man who was *glad* to see the king, the head of whose herald he had taken off (8)? Jesus spoke to Pilate, but not to Herod (9). There is no use talking to some people. This flippant fool is left to his fate.

See the priests *straining every nerve* to secure a verdict against Jesus (10). How earnest devilry can be! What piled infamy and agony are in verse 11! And now, heathenism and Judaism unite against Christianity; enemies become friends at the expense of the Saviour of the world (12). We had better not talk, but think and pray.

Thought: Power is never so great as when restrained.

Luke 23:13-25

Verdicts

The second trial before Pilate (13-25). What a passage this is! The two principals in the scene are condemned, one by the other, and the other by himself; one innocently, and the other justly; one plainly and openly, and the other ignorantly, but certainly. The most condemned man that day was Pilate. He was supposed to be the governor, but he was the governed; the crowd *prevailed* (23). He was cruel, yet not a Nero.

Three times he tried to set Jesus free (4,14,22). He knew perfectly well that his prisoner was innocent. Then why did he not let him go? Because his own deeds in Palestine would not bear investigation, and if he got across with this Jewish crowd, he might be reported to Tiberius, and by him be called to account; and so his past sins drove him on to new crimes. Is your present mortgaged by your past? Then it is time you had a fair reckoning with your past.

Having most solemnly declared that Jesus was innocent (14,15), Pilate straightway proposes to chastise him by scourging, which cruelty always preceded crucifixion (16,22). That suggestion was fatal. If Jesus was innocent, why scourge him? And if guilty, why release him? Pilate impaled himself on the horns of that dilemma. The Jews seized upon the idea, and called for the full penalty, of which that was a part (21). From now, to the end, Pilate hopelessly flounders. His words have no weight because his soul is not sound.

The frenzy of the crowd is difficult to understand (23). Why all that fury? What had Jesus done amiss? By their rage they were pronouncing sentence on human nature. The farcical trial ends; Jesus is condemned; Barabbas is released; Pilate has sold his soul; and the people are pleased (24,25).

Luke's narrative is the briefest. Read the records of the other evangelists. And if our reading does not send us to our knees, something is wrong.

Thought: He who plays with justice punishes himself.

Luke 23:26-43

The road and the hill

In 22:54 to 23:25 we have the record of the several trials which Jesus underwent before the ecclesiastical and civil authorities. We now behold him *on the way to Calvary* (26-32). We are glad to know that there were *companions of the sorrowful way*; a few men, and many women. Simon from North Africa bore the cross for Jesus, which so soon Jesus was to bear for him; only Simon was under it, and Jesus was on it (26).

The circumstances appealed specially to the women, who, forgetful of themselves, made no effort to conceal their love for and sympathy with Jesus (27). His words to them are tender and instructive (28-31). He was moved by their sympathy, yet he said it was misplaced. They themselves would soon be in need of sympathy, and more. He is thinking of the coming destruction of Jerusalem, of which he had spoken before (21:21-24); and tells how terrible it will be. 'If the Romans act thus to me, the innocent and the holy, what shall be the fate of these guilty Jews?' (Farrar on verse 31).

In that following crowd were two condemned brigands, no doubt carrying their own crosses (32). Barabbas should have been the third, but Jesus took his place. I wonder if Barabbas was in the procession!

With eloquent brevity *the crucifixion* is recorded (33). The accompaniments are given in varying detail by the evangelists. Luke's record is in verses 33-49. Three of the seven sayings from the Cross are recorded by Luke only (34,43,46). What a revelation of human nature is in verses 35-37!

Yet Jesus would be universal king—Hellenism, imperialism, and orientalism being represented by the Greek, Latin, and Hebrew on the cross (38).

Verses 39-43 summarise *the religious history of the world*: against Christ, and for him; unsaved and saved; unrepentant and confessing; perishing and living.

Thought: The cross is the only way to the crown.

Luke 23:44-56

The end

The crucifixion is set before us in verses 33-49. It is difficult to write about it, for so many factors enter into the sufferings of the Saviour. The *physical* aspect of them is unspeakably terrible. The fever which soon set in produced a burning thirst. The increasing inflammation of the wounds in the back, hands, and feet; the congestion of the blood in the head, lungs, and heart; the swelling of every vein; an indescribable oppression; racking pain in the head; the stiffness of the limbs, caused by the unnatural position of the body—all contributed to make crucifixion the most horrible of deaths.

But Jesus' *spiritual* sufferings were worse, for he was bearing the sin of the world on his sinless soul. He was on the cross from 9 a.m. to 3 p.m.; and the great darkness lasted for half that time (44). The rending of the veil told of the end of one dispensation, and the beginning of another. Read Hebrews 9.

The end came for Jesus—not for the other two—at 3 p.m. (46). Mark the confession of the centurion, and compare it with other confessions (47). Revulsion of feeling in the multitude soon set in (48); they had been driven by their rulers to their share in the tragedy.

That addition—*and the women* (49,55,27)—is eloquent. Blessed women, who lavishly poured out the ointment of their sympathy in this cruel hour!

Now follows **the entombment** (50-56). Between 3 and 6 p.m. Joseph obtained and buried Jesus' body (50-53). In the act is revealed his character. Specially mark: *he had not consented* (51). Do you always vote with the majority?

From verse 54 and John 19:31, we learn that that day, beginning at 6 p.m. on Friday, was both the Sabbath and the day of the Passover. The feast was then obsolete, for the lamb had been slain. Don't live in dead institutions.

Thought: Redemption makes possible salvation.

Luke 24:1-12

The empty tomb

The last chapter of Luke's Gospel is in three main parts. The first tells of **the resurrection** (1-12); the second of **the manifestations** (13-49); and the third of **the ascension** (50-53). In the first of these mark *the discovery, the illumination,* and *the report.*

● **The discovery** (1-3). The writer is still speaking about the women (23:55,56). It would appear from a comparison of the records that this is the *third* visit to the sepulchre before 6 o'clock that morning: first Mary Magdalene (John 20:1); second, some companions of hers (Mark 16:1); and third, these women (10). What a discovery! The early morning has always been a time of visions: what discoveries the saints have made while others slept!

● **The illumination** (4-8). These women thought, probably, that the body had been stolen (cf. John 20:13). Hence the need of illumination. What was revealed is now explained, and explained by an appeal to memory (6-8; cf. Matthew 17:23). We would have far less anxiety if we paid more attention to what we have been told; if we kept our memories green. For want of this, how many still are *seeking the living among the dead* (5) or substituting a crucifix for Christ, and ceremony for consecration! Don't live among the tombs, seeing that Christ has triumphed over them.

● **The report** (9-12). Surely the most natural thing to do is to pass on good news; yet, how few do it, with this best of news. We are eloquent on any other topic, but are dumb, too often, concerning the things that matter most. *They returned and told.* But that which they brought was not believed (11). While the unbelievers expected something to happen (Matthew 27:65,66), the disciples did not. That's strange! But Peter will see for himself (12, cf. John 20:3-10). Gospel evidences are all around us. Why not believe?

Thought: Diligent desire is rewarded with discovery.

Luke 24:13-24

Three talk

The second and major part of this wonderful chapter records **the manifestations** (13-49) of which there are two: *on the road to Emmaus* (13-35); *in the upper room* (36-49).

On the road to Emmaus (13-35). It is a perfect story, and I pity the reader who does not feel the thrill of it. It is in several parts: what these two disciples said to Jesus; what he said to them; what they said to each other; and what they said to the apostles; and it is all great 'saying'.

No one could have invented verses 13-24! This man (18) and his companion, possibly his wife, were walking the six and a half miles from Jerusalem to their village (13,33), and were very downhearted (17). There was only one thing to talk about (14). And as they went, a stranger joined them (15,16). They did not change the subject of their conversation, but, without knowing who this man was, enemy or friend, they opened their hearts to him (19-24).

Jesus knew what they had been talking about. He asked neither of these questions (17-19) for information, but to draw them out. In a moment or so, he would tell them what they did not know, and so desperately wanted to. It is true still that the Lord asks in order to tell; he takes in order to give.

How psychologically true to such circumstances are verses 19-24: the mixed emotions of these two; their devotion (19); their heartbreak (20); their shattered hope (21a); their rallying hope (21b-23); their astonishment (22), and their half belief (24). The bad news was too true to be doubted, but this other news seemed too good to be true. Mind, all this was said to a stranger! How his heart must have melted towards them!

These disciples had lost Christ by no fault of their own. If we have lost him the fault is ours. They thought well of Christ (19), yet not well enough; but what they did believe prepared them for the fuller revelation.

Thought: Grow as you go, and go as you grow.

Luke 24:25-35

Self-revealed

We are still considering *the first manifestation* of the risen Lord to disciples recorded in this Gospel (13-35). Cleopas has told the stranger who has joined them on the way to Emmaus what was the burden of his and his companion's heart. It is now the stranger's turn to talk, and oh! what talk! See these three, one on each side of the stranger, tramping along the dusty way, their hearts burning within them as they listened to this never-to-be-forgotten unfolding of the Old Testament.

It was Christ talking about himself, instructing them out of his divine self-consciousness in the deeper meaning of Scriptures with which they were familiar. His use of the Old Testament is the true use. Too much has criticism taken the place of Christology, and too often in a zeal for the text we have missed the truth.

Well, they have reached the door of their home, this man and his wife, and the evening is falling. The stranger began to move on, but they earnestly entreated him to stay the night with them, and he went in (28,29). Think of them having the Lord of Glory to take supper with them in their little home! But, as yet, they knew not who he was (16). This verse seems to imply, not only that they did not recognise him, but also, that they were prevented from so doing. The moment had not come.

But at the supper table, the *holden* eyes were *opened*: they knew him; and he disappeared (31). See them dumbly looking at one another; and when they could speak, it was little they could say (32); but they put on their things again and walked back the six and a half miles to Jerusalem to the upper-room, and when they got there, before they could tell their tale, the apostles burst out with: '*The Lord is risen . . . and hath appeared to Simon*' (34), and then, the two told their story (35). What a night! Has Christ ever thrilled you?

Thought: It is the loving heart that gets the open vision.

Luke 24:36-53

In, out and up

In the upper room (36-49). It would seem that the risen Lord appeared ten times to disciples, here and there: five times on the day of the resurrection, and five times on other days. The appearance to the two disciples on the Emmaus road was the fourth on the resurrection day, and to the eleven in the upper room (36) the fifth. He who had suddenly disappeared from Emmaus, suddenly appeared at Jerusalem. For forty days, there was a miraculous coming and going—nothing material proving any obstruction to his glorified body. Were the Emmaus disciples still with the eleven, and did they see the Lord a second time that night?

It should be observed that in his resurrection body Christ spoke with a human voice, and ate food (36,42,43); also, that this body bore some relation to the old one—indeed, was the old one glorified, for there were the healed wounds (39); and still further, that though he was so changed, yet there was identity (31). All this has an important bearing on our future bodies. How tenderly did the Lord allay the fears of his disciples (36-40), and make them feel at home in his presence (41-43).

Dr. A.T. Robertson distinguishes three *appearances* in this portion: on the day of the resurrection (36-43); much later, at Jerusalem (44-49); and on the fortieth day, Ascension day, on Olivet (50-53). That would make *four appearances* in this chapter.

On the occasion of verses 44-49, Christ repeated the Emmaus road talk. Mark the value which he put upon the Old Testament, and the claim he here makes for himself. This is the gospel which his followers are to preach (47,48), and for the preaching of which they would receive the Holy Spirit (49).

The ascension (50-53). And now the last scene: the *journey*, the *benediction*, the *ascension*, the *adoration*, the *rapture*, the *testimony*. A wonderful record of a wonderful Saviour!

Thought: Every end should be a new beginning.

John's Gospel

Contents

1:1-14	Emmanuel: God with us
1:15-28	Courageous humility
1:29-42	The found begin to find
1:43-51	Fruit under a fig-tree
2:1-12	Jesus and joy
2:13-25	A rope for rogues
3:1-13	A teacher is taught
3:14-24	The infallible test
3:25-36	The two Johns speak about Jesus
4:1-14	Making contact with a soul
4:15-30	Hand-plucked fruit
4:31-42	Seize the present hour
4:43-54	Blessed by believing
5:1-14	Omnipotence meets impotence
5:15-29	The Son, the Father and men
5:30-47	The witnesses
6:1-14	A meal on the mountain
6:15-27	Walking on the water
6:28-40	Material and spiritual bread
6:41-59	Eating him
6:60-71	Sifting souls
7:1-13	The loneliness of Jesus
7:14-24	Not of the schools
7:25-36	Knowing and going
7:37-53	A great day
8:1-20	The divine enigma
8:21-30	The self-revealer
8:31-47	Plain speaking
8:48-59	The eternal in time
9:1-12	Light for darkness
9:13-25	Spiritual blindness
9:26-41	Full illumination
10:1-18	A pastoral portion
10:19-30	Eternal life
10:31-42	Rejected evidence
11:1-16	The death of Lazarus
11:17-31	The two sisters
11:32-46	Life from the dead
11:47-57	A priest prophesies
12:1-19	The guest and the King
12:20-36	A temptation resisted
12:37-50	The success of apparent failure

13:1-17	At a supper
13:18-30	The traitor retires
13:31-38	Intimation of departure
14:1-14	An apocalypse of the Father
14:15-31	The advent and work of the Spirit
15:1-17	Fruitfulness and friendship
15:18-27	The church and the world
16:1-15	The mission of the Spirit
16:16-33	Goodbye
17:1-12	The Saviour prays
17:13-26	The Saviour's prayer
18:1-14	The deadly deed
18:15-27	Two trials
18:28-40	Pilate and his prisoner
19:1-16	The judge self-judged
19:17-30	Calvary
19:31-42	The tomb
20:1-18	The great new beginning
20:19-31	Holy friendship
21:1-14	Night and morning
21:15-25	The end

Introduction

John's Gospel

There is almost universal agreement that the fourth Gospel was written by John, the son of Zebedee, 'the disciple whom Jesus loved' (21:20, see 13:23; 19:26). Otherwise there is no direct reference to John in the Gospel. The writer's intimate knowledge of Palestine in general and Jerusalem in particular (see 18:16), his acquaintance with contemporary Judaism, and the testimony of early tradition all tend to confirm this view.

John's Gospel was the last to be written, as its position in the vast majority of manuscripts suggests. It was probably penned at Ephesus in the last decade of the first century A.D.

By this time the other Gospels were already in circulation, so with three authoritative biographies of Christ available there was no need for slavish duplication, and John himself indicates his selectivity (20:30). Clement of Alexandria describes this Gospel as 'a spiritual Gospel', and certainly there is a theological interest and a concern for interpretation, e.g. miracles are referred to as 'signs', revealing the nature of Christ and his ministry.

Even at this early date, there was a tendency to formalism in the church, which the Gospel seeks to correct. Moreover, heretical tendencies were already apparent, denying or obscuring both the deity and humanity of our Lord. Against this background John insists that Jesus was the Christ, the Son of God, who became truly incarnate, and that spiritual life can be found only by saving belief in him (1:12; 10:10; 20:31, etc.). Not surprisingly, multitudes have found Christ as Saviour by reading this Gospel.

John 1:1-14

Emmanuel: God with us

This priceless Gospel is in five parts as follows: 1. *Prologue* (1:1-18). 2. *The revelation of God to the world as life* (1:19 to 12:50). 3. *The revelation of God to the disciples as light* (13:1 to 17:26). 4. *The revelation of God to the disciples and the world as love* (18:1 to 20:31). 5. *The epilogue* (21:1-25). Mark these divisions in your Bible, and master them.

The Prologue (1:1-18), which looks *back*, is in three distinct paragraphs.

● **The divine revelation of the Word** (1-5): to God (1,2); to creation (3); and to man (4,5). How exhaustless an unfolding! God has spoken only one *Word* but it includes the whole language. Nothing could more plainly declare Christ's *divinity*, *infinity*, and *eternity* than these opening words; walk round them, enter into them, and lie down on them. He who is God and Creator is also Redeemer, the *life* and *light* of men. The *darkness* did not and cannot *overcome* the *light* (5, RV).

● **The historic manifestation of the Word** (6-13). He who *was* from all eternity was manifested in *time*. The Light was *revealed* (6-9); *rejected* (10,11); and *received* (12,13). Everyone must do something with the Light. He who made the world, and was in it, was not known by it (9). He came to his own world, and his own people (the Jews) received him not (11, Greek). Christ is at your door; have you let him in? The Life has come, but the world is still dead: the Light has come, but it is still dark. Are you? Do you prefer a rush-light to the Redeemer? Remember, you may reject the Light, but you cannot quench it (4,5).

● **The human apprehension of the Word** (14-18). Here we have the witness of the *apostles* (14); of the *Baptist* (15); and of the *church* (16-18). Plunge into this ocean of truth. *Truth*, yes, and *grace* (14,17): not the one without the other. Do you prefer grace to truth? Will you today *receive of his fullness* (16)?

Thought: Christianity is based on historic facts.

John 1:15-28

Courageous humility

Here we have *the Baptist's witness to Christ*, and he is never so great as when he is content to be small. John, who was six months older than Jesus, was Mary's second cousin.

- **Verse 15.** John's trumpet gave no uncertain sound. *He who follows was first*. What a sublime paradox! John was the prophet of the Highest, but Jesus was the Son of the Highest (Luke 1:76,32). The one was the *minister*, and the other the *mediator* of the new covenant.

- **Verse 16.** Here the Evangelist is speaking, not the Baptist. Memory is clear and frequent in the words: *'Of his fullness have all we received'*. Do you recall what he did for you in days gone by? *'One grace after another';* so will it be eternally.

- **Verse 17.** *Law* and *grace* are contrasted; but *truth* is not here set over against *error*, but *the former partial revelation*.

- **Verse 18.** The first declaration refers not to *mediate*, but to *immediate* gaze. Venture to look at the sun, and you will turn noon into darkness. But God wanted us to see him, so he appeared in Christ (18b).

- **Verses 19-28.** John's witness to Jesus is magnificent. His prompt and emphatic repudiation of the suggestion that he was the Christ, would seem to imply that he was alive to the temptation which presented itself to honour himself instead of his Master. Deal with your temptations summarily. Don't play with them as a cat does with a mouse, or a queer thing may happen, the mouse may become the cat.

These Pharisees, priests and Levites were curious, but not concerned; they wanted to know, but were not willing to believe. The Baptist was neither Christ, nor Elijah, nor anyone but himself (21). It is better to be a consecrated self than a contemptible shadow. **Verse 23.** The Lord was the *Word* (1), John was content to be the *voice*. **Verses 26,27.** John was a fingerpost, and not the way. Be loyal to Christ.

Thought: Borrowed light is better than original darkness.

John 1:29-42

The found begin to find

It is well when a man knows where his limits fall, and when his main work is done. The stars serve a purpose at midday, but it is not to light the world. Enough if they have done that well during the night. So was it with John. He points to Jesus, and in terms of Old Testament type (29).

Try and think of what is meant by *the sin of the world*, and you will have no doubt about *the need of the Lamb*. The *dove* descended on the *Lamb* (32). How wonderful a thought! Meekness and gentleness met to suffer and to save.

There are several *baptisms* in the New Testament which should be distinguished: two by water, John's and Christ's; and, as here, water-baptism, and Spirit-baptism (33).

Andrew and John the apostle were first of all disciples of the Baptist (37, 40). They who follow what light they have will get more: the disciples of John became disciples of Jesus. Are you a progressive Christian?

Jesus is always on the look-out for disciples (38). He who was seeking them asked them who they were seeking. His answer to their question was, '*Come and . . . see*' (39, cf. verse 46). If you have not come, don't be surprised if you don't see. If Jewish time is referred to in verse 39, it was 4 p.m. when these two men attached themselves to Jesus. John remembered it well after seventy years.

As soon as you are *found by* Christ you should *find for* him. That's what Andrew did (41,42); and his first find was a great one. The goldfields of South Africa are not in it with this discovery! Mark that Andrew began with those nearest to him: he did not start his missionary work *abroad*, but at *home*. Have you an unsaved brother? What a thrill there is in the words, *we have found* (41). The son of a *dove* (Jonah) would become as firm as a *rock* (42). Christ can do wonderful things.

Thought: Activity is the evidence of vitality.

John 1:43-51

Fruit under a fig-tree

This chapter may well be called *eureka*, discovery, for it is full of it. *John the Baptist* finds *Jesus*, Jesus finds *Andrew* and *John* the apostle. Andrew finds *Simon*, Jesus finds *Philip*, and Philip finds *Nathanael*, who is the apostle Bartholomew. Do you know anything about the thrill of spiritual discovery?

Philip now recognised in Jesus the fulfilment of the hopes of devout Israel alike in law and prophecy (45). His friend could not at once credit that (46a). Nazareth is not so much as named in the Old Testament; was it possible, then, that the Christ should emerge from there, and not from Zion, city of their God?

Nathanael had to learn, as we have, that Christ may appear where he is least expected. He is willing today to reside in humble souls, as long ago he was willing to dwell in humble towns. Philip was neither philosopher nor dialectician, but a plain man, who believed, and so his answer to this thinker was, '*Come and see*' (46). That ends all argument regarding Christ. Put him to the proof. Philip learned that answer from Christ himself (39).

No one starts Christward whom Christ does not see, whom he did not see before that one started (47a, 48b). Nathanael was a good man when Jesus found him, and he soon became a better man: everyone must, in Jesus' company. Jesus could not say of him that he had *no guilt*, but he did say that he had *no guile*; but Christ can make us both guiltless and guileless. Hallelujah!

How great is Nathanael's confession which follows! (49). He goes all the way, and proclaims him man, God and king. Faith is always rewarded (50, 51). He who sees the spiritual visible, will soon see the spiritual invisible. There's an open way between earth and heaven, and holy traffic thereon.

Thought: Christ always says the best he can of us.

John 2:1-12

Jesus and joy

The third day from the last day mentioned (1:43), Jesus, his mother, and his disciples, three, or possibly four in number, attended a wedding. As God founded marriage (Genesis 2), it is fitting that he should attend a wedding. Almost certainly Joseph was dead by now—hence the mention of Mary only (1).

Did you invite Jesus to your wedding? He never is an unbidden guest. When you begin to build a home, be sure and have a good foundation. The great symbols are a cradle, a school, a church, wedding-bells, and a grave. Have Christ with you in all the crises of your life. So far as we know, this was the first marriage which Jesus attended, but not the last. There is one yet to come (Revelation 19:7).

The wine failed, but Jesus did not (3). We can get on without wine, but not without him. Mary's observation was intercession (3). What Jesus means by his reply is, 'I have now entered upon my divine work, and my actions henceforth are directed from within, are independent of all without.' Mary had to learn this (4), and did learn it (5).

Christ's was a planned life; there were no idle hours in it; he was never at a loose end (4b). When the moment came to supply the want, it was done lavishly. Jesus provided the party with not less than 120 gallons of wine (6).

In this, the ordinary course of nature was not suspended, but precipitated. The rain became red; the water became a wonder. After all, grapes in six months are as surprising as wine in six moments. To say that miracles are impossible is ridiculous. What *are* miracles?

'*Thou hast kept the good wine until now*' (10). After the law, the gospel, and the best came last. *The sower* is the first of the parables: this is the first of the *signs* (11). Christ's parables were miracles in words; his miracles were parables in deeds.

Verse 12. The family life was not yet broken.

Thought: Give Christ room and time to help you.

John 2:13-25

A rope for rogues

From 2:13 to 4:54, we see *Jesus at work*, first in *Judea* (2:13 to 3:36), then, in *Samaria* (4:1-42), and then, in *Galilee* (4:43-54). The narrative which tells how he relates himself to a *man*, a *woman*, and a *child*, is led up to by this passage.

Christ commenced and concluded his ministry by a judicial act (13-17; Matthew 21:12,13).

The Temple was still the *Father's house* (16), but soon it was to become the house of the unbelieving nation (Matthew 23:38). Westcott points out the difference between two words translated *temple* in the AV: *hieron*, meaning the whole sacred enclosure, with the courts and the porticoes; and *naos*, the actual sacred building. The former word is in verses 14, 15; and the latter, in verses 19-21.

This incident (14-16) is a warning against secularizing the sacred, against degrading the divine, against commercializing the church. You do not need to bring a beast within its borders in order to do that; you do it by cherishing the spirit of these Jews. There is a heresy of spirit far too common in sacred acts and places.

Jesus did not drive out these traders by violence, but by authority; of this the cord-scourge was the symbol. Of what do your actions remind people (17)? Divine justice is divine love in flames. All may share the Saviour's zeal, but may not, like him, take up the scourge. How fearsome a thing is wrathful love!

These Jews wanted to justify a sign by a sign (18). Stupid. What opposite thoughts may circle round the same word or words (19-21)! Jesus was talking about *his body*; they were talking about *their building*.

In verse 17 is history that once was prophecy; in verse 22 is prophecy that soon would become history. In verses 23-25, the people's fake-faith is searched by Christ's perfect insight.

Thought: He who is incapable of anger cannot love.

John 3:1-13

A teacher is taught

This story of *Nicodemus* is immediately connected with what goes before. Many appeared to trust Jesus, but he did not trust himself to them, because, knowing all men, he knew that they were only sign-saints (2:23-25). But there were exceptions. There always are. In 1 Corinthians 1:26, it does not say 'not *any*', but 'not *many*'; there always are some sincere seekers after the Saviour, and they find the Saviour who is seeking them. Nicodemus did (7:50,51; 19:39).

We would never have heard of Nicodemus if he had never come to Jesus. How many more men and women we would have heard of if they had only come. Every man in the Gospels appears in the light reflected on him from the Lord. This man's social position and office rendered his salvation a problem, but the *Pharisee* was pardoned, and the *teacher* (10) was taught. His curiosity led to concern, and concern led to conversion. That is often the history of the great change.

This is the greatest passage on *the new birth* in the Bible. Salvation is not by labour or culture, but by regeneration; it is not a reformation, but a new creation. No one can understand it, but all may experience it (8). Christianity is not a philosophy, but a life; it expresses itself not in terms of logic, but of love; it is not living the old life in a new way, but being born into a new life. Apart from this *new birth* no one can even *see* the kingdom of God, let alone *enter into* it (3,5).

Nicodemus asks, *How?* Jesus answers, *Except.* It would seem that Jesus in verse 5 is referring to John's baptism, not of course as a means of regeneration, but as a preparation for it in the way of repentance. There is only one door of entrance into this kingdom. Have you entered in?

Thought: Learn how to live, for darkness is death.

John 3:14-24

The infallible test

In verses 1-15 is the momentous conversation between Jesus and the ruler, but in verses 16-21 we have, in all likelihood, the words, not of Jesus, but of John. Study carefully verses 14, 15. There is enough truth here, with verse 16, to save the world. What is needed today is not light from God, but faith from men. Christ has died. Sinners believe. 'Lifted up was he to die; "It is finished," was his cry. Now in heaven exalted high, Hallelujah! What a Saviour!'

Mark the two '*musts*' in this passage. The Son *must* be lifted up (14); the sinner *must* be born again (7). Have you ever tried to imagine what it is for a soul to *perish* (15)? Don't take a risk on that. Of verse 16, Luther says, 'These words are the Bible in miniature,' and when dying, he repeated them.

The greatness of God's love is seen in its object, plan, agent, manifestation, conditions, disinterestedness, and results. When Nott assured the Tahitians that this verse was true, they said, 'And canst thou speak of such love without tears?'

The moral element in belief or unbelief is prominent in verses 16-21. Men can, and should, believe. If they do not, they place themselves under condemnation (18). If we do not enter into light, it is because we prefer darkness (19). Truth is not something to be intellectually believed, but to be dynamically performed (20).

Though by Christ's coming the world is condemned, yet, he did not come to condemn the world. The *effect* is one thing; the *purpose* is another (17). *Saved* in this verse is the opposite of *perish* in verse 15. The sinner's *judgement* is *already* recorded, but not yet executed. What you *love* is character-determining (19).

The *evil-doing* in verse 20 refers, not to a single act of guilt, but to habit, to persistent practice of wrong: '*This is the test by which men are judged*' (Weymouth). What we really believe, we do; our actions reflect our character; and according to character is destiny.

Thought: Where there is not faith there must be failure.

John 3:25-36

The two Johns speak about Jesus

A careful examination of this passage will surely lead to the conclusion that whereas verses 27-30 are the words of John the Baptist, verses 31-36 are those of John the Evangelist, as, almost certainly, are verses 16-21. The occasion of the Baptist's utterance is stated in verses 25, 26. This *question about purifying* had reference, in all likelihood, to the religious value of John's baptism, in the light of the baptism which Jesus' disciples administered (22; 4:1,2). Maybe the thought had arisen that John and Jesus were rivals.

This situation was for John both a temptation and an opportunity; a temptation to exalt himself, and an opportunity to magnify Christ; and he did the latter (27-30). The Baptist stood to Jesus in the relation of the *best man* to the bridegroom at a present-day wedding. Such a one makes preparation for the great event, *stands* to serve, and *hears* to obey the bridegroom's wishes (29). With the celebration of the marriage the *best man* ceases to function; he drops out. This is what John did (30).

The Evangelist's reflections on the relationship between the Baptist and Jesus (31-36) were written between sixty and seventy years after that of which he speaks, and he affirms that the Baptist's witness had been fulfilled. The words, *from above* and *of the earth* (31), have not a moral significance, but point to *origin*. Plainly, it means, Jesus was *divine*, whereas the Baptist was *human*. We do not believe that what God says is true unless we accept Christ's testimony (33). *Put his seal to* means *solemnly declared*.

In verse 34 *God* and *unto him* are not in the original text so that the reference may be to God's or Christ's bestowal of the Spirit. The important point is that the Spirit is fully given. Have you received him fully? Do you know God *as Father* (36a), or only *as God* (36b)? It matters.

Thought: The best leadership is to follow Christ.

John 4:1-14

Making contact with a soul

Verses 1-3 introduce what follows in verses 4-42. Several points here should not be overlooked. For instance, the use of *Lord* and *Jesus*. The latter was what the Pharisees knew him to be; the former, what John knew him to be. What do you know him to be? How much is he to you?

Then, notice the correction of a report (2). This is John's aside, as are also verse 8, and the last sentences of verse 9. The baptism of preparation was the work of the herald, not of the king. Christian baptism presupposes the death and resurrection of Christ.

Again, Jesus' movements were affected by circumstances (1, 3). None of us can say what he will do tomorrow, because none of us knows what circumstances may arise. Herein is the necessity for divine guidance.

In chapter 3 Jesus' conversation was with a man; here, it is with a woman. There, the person is honourable; here, disreputable. There the talk circled round regeneration; here, round worship. There, the appeal was made to understanding; here to conscience. There, to a Jew; but here to a Gentile. Study our Lord's interviews with women, recorded in the Gospels.

Mark the natural in this story so full of the supernatural. He who claimed to be the Christ of age-long prophecy and hope (25) was *tired* by walking, and needed rest (6). Why should the Creator stand on convention (9, 27)? Jesus' course was determined, not by whether persons were men or women, Jews or Gentiles, but by their need. So should it be with us.

As before Nicodemus and Jesus both spoke of *birth*, but in different senses (3:3,4), so here, the woman and Jesus both speak of *water*, but in different senses (13, 14). Distinguish *well* (*phrear*, 12) and *fountain* (*pege*, 14). He who wills eternally to quench the sinner's thirst, would not quench his own on Calvary (14). '*Art thou greater?*' (12). Yes. He is greater, the greatest of the great.

Thought: Always be ready for opportunity.

John 4:15-30

Hand-plucked fruit

These verses complete the conversation which was begun in verse 7. This woman, without granting the request made of her (7), asks for a favour of Jesus (15); and he satisfied her thirst, though she did not satisfy his. Of course, he always does more for us than we do for him, but do we do all we can?

Very much may be learned from this story on the subject of *method in soul winning*. Jesus never dealt with any two people in just the same way, and simply because no two people are precisely alike. In his service we are dealing with souls and not with stock.

What a collision of ideas is in verses 15, 16! On the woman's interpretation of *thirst* and *water*, the answer of Jesus is altogether irrelevant, but not on his interpretation of them. He was speaking of what was spiritual, and would have her and us know that the spiritual is conditioned by and issues in the ethical. In other words, *no one who is wrong with his fellows can be right with God*. Do you believe that?

Impurity is certainly impiety. The woman's answer was an attempt to dodge the thrust (17a). but there is no escape from Christ (17b, 18). He knows, and we had better flee to his knowledge than narcotise our conscience.

Again the woman makes for escape, by raising a standing issue between Jews and Samaritans (19, 20). The *mountain* referred to is Gerizim (Deuteronomy 27:12). Well, as the woman had opened up the *worship* avenue, Jesus approached her along that line. He says, in effect, that worship of God is reality, not religiosity. Judaism was a worship of the letter, and not of *spirit*: Samaritanism was a worship of falsehood, and not of *truth*; but true worship is '*in spirit and in truth*' (24).

Jesus now gives concreteness to this woman's vague hope (25, 26). Day dawned in her soul, and she went right home and confessed (28, 29). Tell what you know.

Thought: Every soul may be saved.

John 4:31-42

Seize the present hour

Jesus had spoken of *spiritual birth*, and Nicodemus thought the reference was to natural birth. Again, Jesus had spoken of *spiritual water*, and the woman of Samaria imagined that he spoke of the water in the well. And now, Jesus speaks of *spiritual food*, and his disciples suppose that he tells of physical nourishment which he has received (31-33). In all history has anyone been more misunderstood than Christ?

Do we believe that obedience to God's will is food (34)? We cannot work unless we eat; so *Jesus feeds on God's will that he may finish his work* (34).

In our next paragraph (35-38) are several great lessons:

● *We should see in the present what we look for in the future* (35). Some people who praise the past, and look to the future with hope, seem to despair only of the present. Are you looking for a harvest in months to come? Look, the fields are already white.

● *All labour for God is rewarded* (36). We should be more concerned about the quality of our work for him than about its particular class. Some are sowers, and others are reapers, but all should be good sowers and reapers.

● *All Christian service is co-operative* (37, 38). We are not competitors, but co-workers. There are many departments in a great factory, and many processes go to the making of a single article, but the workers are not rivals; they all have one end in view. So is it in the service of our Lord. Then, let us drop our jealousies and proud criticisms.

The third paragraph (39-42) tells of *the creation of faith mediately* (39), *and immediately* (42). To go from the woman to Jesus was to advance; but no one went from Jesus to the woman. There is no need to drink down the stream if we have access to the fountain. Have you heard him yourself? And do you know (42)? Faith must be in *his* Word (41).

Thought: Do not go to heaven empty-handed.

John 4:43-54

Blessed by believing

The Christian witness is all inclusive; first in *Judea* (chapter 3), then, in *Samaria* (4:1-42), and now, in *Galilee* (4:43-54). Palestine was a microcosm, and the spread of the evangel throughout all its borders was prophetic of worldwide evangelisation, as the capture of representatives of all classes – a ruler, a harlot, a nobleman, a Jew, a Samaritan, a Roman – was prophetic of the great multitude which no man can number – of all nations, and peoples, and tongues – who would wash their robes, and make them white in the blood of the Lamb. Think about that.

Physical diseases are the shadows of spiritual ills, and Christ's will and power to heal the one, tell of his ability to heal the other. In that view we see that not only are *men* (Nicodemus), and *women* (the Samaritan) in need of salvation, but also *children* (46). Boys and girls inherit the nature of their parents, and if the latter need to be saved, so do the former. It is well when parents show the concern for their children's spiritual welfare which this man did for his son's recovery (47, 49); and well also, when they exercise a like faith in the power, will, and promise of the Lord (50).

The proverb says, '*Seeing is believing*,' but the Bible says that we should *believe to see*. This man did.

Are your children Christians? If not, are you at all responsible? If you cannot bring them to Jesus, you can at least go to Jesus about them. This son was too sick to bring, but the father was well enough to go. But of course, sick parents cannot even go about their sick children. If you would allure them to brighter worlds, you must 'lead the way'.

Compare and contrast Christ's two miracles in Cana (54, 46; 2:1). Without Jesus, the one would scarcely have been a feast, and the other would certainly have been a funeral; but he is at once the bringer of joy and the banisher of sorrow. He meets each of us at the point of our need.

Thought: He only is noble who does nobly.

John 5:1-14

Omnipotence meets impotence

With chapter 5 opens a distinct section in the narrative of our Lord's public ministry. Up to now faith has dominated, but from now unbelief prevails. Jesus' miracles are the occasions of the increasing opposition: the healing of the impotent man, also of the man born blind, and the raising of Lazarus. How strange that help should be made the occasion of hate, and blessing the occasion of blasphemy! Yet so it was, and so it often is. Omit the words from *waiting* (3) to *he had* (4), which are an early uninspired note, designed to explain verse 7.

This chapter divides into three parts: *the sign* (1-9), *the sequel* (10-18), and *the sermon* (19-47). The whole chapter is peculiar to John.

What a picture we have in verse 3, of the waste of humanity; '*a great multitude*', with all sorts of troubles. Here is scope for the Saviour. Of all these people one is brought into prominence, as well he might be after having been impotent for thirty-eight years. Three points will summarise this story, namely, Jesus' *question*, and *command*, and *warning* (6, 11, 14).

One would have thought that the first and third of these should not have been necessary. Does not everyone wish to be made whole? Would anyone sin when such consequences follow? Alas, most people do not wish for spiritual health, and multitudes continuously sin, regardless of consequences, grieving only for the results, not the causes.

What utter triflers these Jews were (10)! What better day than the Sabbath on which to bring deliverance to body or soul! Some people are more concerned about convention than conversion; have more regard for tradition than for truth. Bondage to the externals of religion has always been a curse.

In verse 14, Jesus warns this man against a relapse; physically dangerous, but spiritually it may easily prove fatal. See Hebrews 10:26.

Thought: There is hope for people in middle life.

John 5:15-29

The Son, the Father and men

If by telling the Jews that it was Jesus who had healed him, this man expected to commend his benefactor, how sadly disappointed he must have been (15, 16)! These sticklers for the Sabbath would not stick at murder; they would keep the day, but kill the deliverer. Can you understand that state of mind?

Mark carefully Jesus' answer to the Jews' antagonism (17). Westcott has well said: 'The rest of God after the creation, which the Sabbath represents outwardly, and which Christ came to realise, is not a state of inaction, but of activity: and man's true rest is not a rest *from* human earthly labour, but a rest *for* divine heavenly labour. Thus the merely negative, traditional, observance of the Sabbath is placed in sharp contrast with the positive final fulfilment of spiritual service for which it was a preparation.'

After this, the Jews would kill Jesus for what he had *said* (18) as well as for what he had *done* (16). What he had done was wholly good, and what he had said was wholly true. Then, why want to get rid of him?

The discourse which follows is profound.

● First, Jesus speaks of *his relation to the Father* (19-23). Mark the four times repeated *for* (19, 20, 21, 22). Here we learn of the Son's *subordination* to the Father (19), his *fellowship* with the Father (20), his *equality* with the Father (21, 23), and his *commission* from the Father (22).

● Next Jesus speaks of *his relation to men* (24-29). Verse 24 is great. Salvation is based on the human side, on knowledge and faith. 'He who knows the gospel and knows that the gospel is true, cannot but have life.' Mark carefully, *hath life . . . is passed*. How glad the certainty! Distinguish between Christ's reference to *present spiritual resurrection* (25) and *future physical resurrection* (28). We're not done with when we're dead: we have a future of weal or of woe (29).

Thought: Today will largely determine tomorrow.

John 5:30-47

The witnesses

From verse 20, in this discourse, it is noticeable that Jesus makes a change in his reference to himself. From verses 19-29 the reference is indirect: *the Son*; but from verses 30-47, it is direct: *I*. The subject of this second part of the discourse is: **witness to the Son**, and Jesus speaks first of the witness borne (31-40) and then, of the witness rejected (41-47).

The witness borne (31-40). Five voices of witness are heard.

- *The witness of Christ himself* (31). With this verse compare 8:14. This is not a contradiction. The former refers to the witness of Christ himself *alone*; the latter, to his witness as authorised by and dependent on the Father (8:16,18).

- *The witness of the Baptist* (32-35). Jesus always spoke well of John. Can he of you? The herald did not speak about himself, but of his Master. He was a *lamp*, and not the *light*. All human lamps go out, but the light continues to shine.

- *The witness of the works* (36). What one does is a revelation of what one is; and the character of our accomplishment will disclose the source of our inspiration.

- *The witness of the Father* (37,38). Jesus here declares that not to believe him is to remain in ignorance of the Father.

- *The witness of the Scriptures* (39, 40). Read, 'Ye search the Scriptures.' It is an affirmation, not an exhortation.

The witness rejected (41-47). But alas, this manifold witness was, and is, rejected. Of such an attitude we here see the *cause* (41-44), and *end* (45-47). In its essence the cause is found in *love of self* instead of *love of God*, and the end of rejecting Christ is that men are condemned by that to which they looked for justification (45-47). He who refuses the witness of Christ's messengers refuses Christ. Is your minister a prophet? Then pay attention to what he says. Verse 47 declares the inspiration of the Old Testament.

Thought: Christ's claims are sovereign.

John 6:1-14

A meal on the mountain

The two accounts of the feeding of a crowd are not variations of one event, but are of two distinct miracles, each having its own lessons to teach. Compare and contrast these.

In the previous chapter Christ revealed himself as the *giver* of life; here, he reveals himself as the *sustainer* of life. In the one, we should mark his relation to the *Father*, and in the other, his relation to the *believer*.

Westcott divides this chapter into three parts; *the signs* (1-21); *the discourses* (22-59); *the issue* (60-71).

There are two signs, and here our attention is called to the first: *the feeding of the 5,000*. Of the eight miracles which John records, this one is found in the other three Gospels, and the next one (15-21) in Matthew and Mark; the other six are recorded by John only. Make a list of them.

Nearly a year of ministry has elapsed between chapters 5 and 6. There, Jesus was in Jerusalem; here, he is in *Galilee*. This is the only portion of the Galilean ministry related by John. This narrative reveals Christ's *compassion* as well as his *power*, and the former before the latter.

It also shows that while Christ's first concern is the souls of men, he is not indifferent to *the needs of our bodies*. Some who satisfy their stomachs starve their souls. Feeding the poor can never be a substitute for preaching the gospel to them. Well, circumstances are tests (6), and one who may appear to be mentally fertile when the larder is full, may be found to be mentally bankrupt when it is empty (7).

We have here an interesting start for the study of *Philip* and *Andrew*. Great parts have been played by unnamed children in the history of the world (9). This feast was not a scramble; the Lord would teach us a lesson on *decorum* and *order* (10). He would also teach us to offer *thanks to God* for the least of his gifts (11). Is he acknowledged at *your* table? And further, Jesus would teach us a lesson on *economy* (12, 13).

Thought: The fed should feed the famishing.

John 6:15-27

Walking on the water

The second sign is *Christ walking on the sea* (15-21). Oftentimes, in certain circumstances, Jesus did just the opposite of what any of us would have done. If we knew that people were coming to crown us, we would let them, but Jesus *departed*.

This sea scene is very impressive. The fear of these fishermen is surprising. Surely they had been in many a storm. It is a sad thing for any Christian to be in the dark without Christ; in the dark of doubt, of sorrow, of loss (17). But let no one at such a time imagine that the Master has forgotten. When he seems furthest removed from us, he is praying for us (Matthew 14:22,23), and in the crisis of our need he will appear (19).

No one can altogether escape storm on life's sea, and it is better to be in a storm with Christ than in a calm without him. Listen for that word of assurance above the howl of the tempest: *I am* (20, Greek). Nine times in John does Jesus claim this Jehovah name. Trace them.

Jesus was never left alone for long; there were always people at his heels, but more for the temporalities than the spiritualities (22-24). In answer to the question of some (25), Jesus enters upon this long *discourse*, which may be divided into four distinct dialogues; verses 25-40, 41-51, 52-59 and 60-65.

The motives of the crowd must have been a real disappointment to Jesus (26). When Henry Martyn was discouraged because the Hindus at Dinapore came only for rice, he read this verse, and was cheered. That Christ suffered as we do, should be a help when we are inclined to think that no one has ever had our trouble.

Lange says verse 27 contains a double paradox: that they should not labour for the perishable food, which they had to do to live; and that they should labour for the heavenly food, which is not to be earned by labour.

Thought: Christ would be nearer to us if he were dearer to us.

John 6:28-40

Material and spiritual bread

Attention should be paid to *Jesus' method of teaching*. Generally the *instruction* grew out of some *circumstance* with which he was dealing, and that circumstance was made the text of the address. In chapter 3 it was *birth*; in chapter 4 it was *water*; here it is *bread*; in chapter 10 it is *sheep*; and so on. Jesus' miracles were acted parables, and his parables were spoken miracles.

The key to the present discourse is verse 35. How profoundly we should be impressed by Jesus' claims for himself. How anyone can read such a discourse as this, and doubt that he was the eternal Son of God, passes my comprehension.

To believe on Christ is not a reverie; it is a *work* (29). How little did the people understand who Jesus was! What was the falling of manna from heaven in comparison with the coming of the Manna therefrom (30-35)? Consider Heber's hymn: 'Bread of the world, in mercy broken, Wine of the soul, in mercy shed, By whom the words of life were spoken, And in whose death our sins are dead'.

The teaching of Jesus is full of paradoxes. For example, put verse 35 by the side of Matthew 5:6. The whole of the truth about anything cannot be fixed in any one phrase. The sublimest truth is often found in sharp contradictions. Think about that!

It is said that *seeing is believing*, but these people saw and did *not* believe (36).

Make a note of the two great truths in verse 37: *divine election*, and *eternal security*. In verse 38 Christ acknowledges his mediatorial subordination to the Father. Compare *lose nothing* in verse 39 with *that nothing be lost* in verse 12.

Connect the four occurrences of '*I will raise him up at the last day*,' a phrase found only in this Gospel. Christ's consciousness of vocation was ever strong and sensitive (40). He knew the present, and he also saw clearly the future.

Thought: Bread is not for criticism, but for consumption.

John 6:41-59

Eating him

The second (41-51), and third (52-59) parts of this *discourse* touch on the greatest mysteries of Christ's life: the incarnation and the atonement (42,51); and the greatest mysteries of man's life: the concurrence of the divine and human will, and the permanence of life (44,45,47).

If these Jews had known who Jesus was, whence he came would not have constituted a problem for them. It is misunderstanding that provokes murmur. Jesus insists on his unique and vital relation to God the Father.

Study each reference to *the Father* in this discourse. Christ's supreme revelation was of the Father, and that revelation was made in the Son's own person. God can be known in many ways, but the Father, in only one way. How infinite the distance between *my Father* (32), and *your fathers* (49)!

Verses 53-58 do not refer only or primarily to the Lord's Supper, for one may partake of that without doing what is here written; and one may do what is here written without partaking of the Lord's Supper. These mystical words tell of the believer's appropriation and assimilation of Christ, and this is done by faith.

Sacraments apart from faith are a mockery, and faith is valid without sacraments. There are many in heaven who never communed, and, it is to be feared, many in hell who often did. The apprehension of the meaning of these words of our Lord must be spiritual rather than intellectual. Augustine says, 'Let us be content to adore while others dispute.'

Our Lord's references to *manna* in this discourse show us that the experiences and institutions of Israel of old were typical, and further, that he himself is the fulfilment of many of these types. Jesus' profoundest discourses are recorded in this Gospel, because it is written for the church. Let us not desire to bring down its truths to the level of our understanding, but pray that our understanding may be raised to the level of its truths.

Thought: Sympathy is insight.

John 6:60-71

Sifting souls

The key to the interpretation of what has preceded is found in verse 63. Words are only the embodiment of ideas, and must always prove inadequate for the expression of the greatest ideas. This is not a discourse that lends itself to literalism, but to the insight which is begotten of fellowship with the redeeming Lord. Of course these *many disciples* (60) could not understand such a message, because they *believed not* (64). This, of course, does not refer to the twelve (67), except Judas (64,70,71).

The blind often pass through most glorious country, but they see it not. As little can the unconverted understand this discourse. There is no sight where there is no life. But be it said, there may be sight without insight.

Peter, however, had insight on this occasion (68,69). What is called the great confession of Peter, in Matthew 16:16, was made after this, and in almost identical terms. If you who profess Christ forsake him, *to whom will you go*? (68). To lifeless formalism? To vain superstitions? To cold morality? To ruinous worldliness? If, like Peter, you *are sure* of Christ, there will be no turning back; this, however, is not the sureness of a mathematical calculation, but of faith's most daring venture.

Judas is an insoluble mystery. How such a man could have continued in the company of Jesus is difficult to understand, but it is far more difficult to understand why Jesus ever chose him (70). Judas is the most tragic moral ruin in human history. The man who ate and slept and walked and talked with Jesus for probably two years, who heard his teaching, witnessed his miracles, and beheld his sinless character, sold him for a pittance.

He is the only man whom Jesus called *a devil* (70). Others *had* devils, but Judas *was* one. From the beginning Jesus knew this, yet suffered him. That is love beyond compare.

Thought: Open opposition is better than feigned friendship.

John 7:1-13

The loneliness of Jesus

This chapter is in three main parts: *before the feast* (1-13); *during the feast* (14-36); and *the last day of the feast* (37-52).

The record of chapter 6 tells of what happened in the Spring, March — April; chapters 7,8 tell of events in the Autumn, September — October; so that there is a period of six months between chapter 6 and chapter 7, of which John has no record. In this gap put Matthew 12 to 17.

Before the feast (1-13)
I would call your attention to three things in this passage.

1. *Jesus had a difficult time at home* (3-5). By *his brethren* is meant his brothers, sons of Joseph and Mary, two of whom, James, and Jude, afterward wrote Holy Scripture.

Now, when we remember that Jesus was in the Nazareth home for over thirty years, and saw this family grow up; when we remember that in his boyhood's days he became conscious of who he really was, and yet performed the daily task, keeping the great secret to himself; when we remember that he lived through all these years a perfect life, and set an example which might well have caused the family to think; and when we remember what claims he publicly made for himself when once he had entered upon his great mission, we shall readily understand how keenly he must have felt it that his brethren did not believe in him. But unbelief gave way to faith after the resurrection (1 Corinthians 15:7).

2. *Jesus' life was a plan of God* (6,8). His schedule was determined in heaven. He worked by an unseen clock. For everything there was an 'hour', and as he never was before his time, so he never was behind.

3. *Jesus was a subject of sharp controversy* (12). He certainly was very good, or very bad. Let nineteen hundred years of his influence say which. He who wears black glasses will see the sun black, but he who wears clear glasses would not see a black sun golden. Oh, no; the facts are against unbelievers.

Thought: When thought is straight, life will be strong.

John 7:14-24

Not of the schools

We now enter upon what happened **during the feast** (14-36).

● *Scene one* (14-24)
Jesus did not dissociate himself from Temple and synagogue; we find him constantly there (14); by which we may learn that we should not neglect the appointed means of grace (Hebrews 10:25).

But the ecclesiastics and theologians of that day were astonished at the success of one who had not graduated at any of their seminaries (15). As it was, so it is.

To think that a preacher has no standing unless he has the stamp of a university or college, is pure intellectual snobbery. Where did Bunyan train, and Spurgeon, and Moody? What degrees had they? I know of *a good degree* which no college has it in its power to give (1 Timothy 3:13).

Don't misunderstand: the more knowledge a man can acquire, the better; the intellectual house of every preacher should be well furnished. But what's the good of that in midwinter if there's not a fire in the grate? Give me a room with one chair in it, and a good fire, rather than every luxury of furniture with the temperature at freezing point.

The supreme need of the hour is not for academicians, but apostles; not pundits, but prophets; not scholars, but saints; not experts, but evangelists. The former will always have their work to do, and if they can also be the latter, they will be well-nigh invincible, but if a choice has to be made in the interests of the gospel, we do not hesitate.

The *one work* referred to in verse 21, you will find in 5:1-9 (23). When will people learn that neither slander nor stones ever accomplished anything good yet (19,20)? To call a man by ugly names does not make him ugly, and to kill a good man is not to get rid of him. Jesus met their ribaldry with reason (21-24).

Thought: When knowledge weds power, the offspring will be good.

John 7:25-36

Knowing and going

In the controversy **during the feast** (14-36), there are three scenes, in each of which the thoughts of a group of people are disclosed. In scene one, of the Jews (14-24); in scene two, of 'some of the inhabitants of Jerusalem' (25-31); and in scene three, of the envoys of 'the chief priests and the Pharisees' (32-36). The last two of these scenes are in this passage.

● *Scene two* (25-31).
Some people seem to have been born in the objective case, for they are fertile in fault-finding and clever at criticism. Students of the Greek New Testament should mark the two words for *know* in verse 27: *oida*, objective knowledge, and *ginosko*, subjective knowledge. If people only knew how ignorant they were, they would not boast of a knowledge which they do not possess. These people's *whence* was Nazareth, not Bethlehem. Had they never read Micah 5:2?

In Jesus' reply, as in many passages, his consciousness of *origin* and *mission* is made very plain (28,29). None other in the world's history has ever had such a consciousness. Man's power is impotent until God allows him to exercise it (30). Compare verse 30b with 13:1. The people of verse 31 were in a state of incipient faith; they were approaching the truth, but did not actually arrive. You, too, may be on the margin of a great discovery, so go just a little further.

● *Scene three* (32-36).
Jesus definitely announces his imminent departure. This should impress us more than it does. The future, as well as the past, was known to Jesus. He knew not only *that* he was going to leave this world, but also *when*, and *how*. But how did he know all that? You do not know the course of today, not to say tomorrow, but Christ did, *because he was Christ*. What Jesus said to these people was utterly incomprehensible (35,36). Do you understand what he says to you? Listen today.

Thought: Rest in Christ's knowledge, and follow his lead.

John 7:37-53

A great day

The Feast of Tabernacles moved towards a climax, and so, **the last day of the feast** was the 'great day'. This was the last of the three great feasts in Israel. *Passover* celebrated the deliverance from Egypt; *Pentecost* commemorated the giving of the law; and *Tabernacles* revealed God's goodness to his people while they were in the wilderness.

Well, when the great day of this great feast arrived, Jesus made for himself a great *claim*, and issued a great *promise* (37-39). The claim was, that he was the satisfier of the souls of men; and the promise was wrapped up in the claim, as the comment of the apostle makes plain (39); it was the promise of the Holy Spirit.

The order of experience is *thirst, come, drink, flow*; an order which is never reversed. *Living water* tells of the quality of the blessing received; *rivers* tells of the copiousness of it; and *flow* tells of the sharing of it with others. We must be full if we would flow, for others are blessed only by our overflow.

Observe that the same testimony makes opposite impressions on different people (40-44). The difference was in the hearers and not in the speaker. The same sun which melts wax, hardens clay. See 2 Corinthians 2:15,16. How do you react to Christ?

Read verse 44, and ask *Why?* For the answer, see verse 30. We see from verse 45 that an evil design had not matured (32). Since then, some who went to church to scoff, have remained to pray. Opposers of Christianity have also the Holy Spirit to reckon with. No doubt these Pharisees were sincere, but sincerity can be very wicked (45-49). Sincerity, to be safe, must be enlightened. But all occasions are tests.

This occasion tested Nicodemus, and he did not fail (50,51). Turn up the reference to him before this, and the one after. Verse 53 and 8:1 go together. What a lot of muddled thinking there is (41,42,52)!

Thought: The flow is only from the fountain.

John 8:1-20

The divine enigma

What all men need is *life*, and *light*, and *bread*, and *water*, and in this Gospel Christ claims to be all these. Because spiritually we, like the woman taken in adultery, are by nature dead, and dark, and starved, we need Christ. Saul was once in darkness at midday, and so are we all, and always, until we receive Christ.

By '*the light of life*' (12) is meant the light which both springs from, and issues in, life. Being the light, Christ, of course, shone, and yet these men said that the light was not to be trusted *because* it was shining (13). The tortuous thinking of some people is difficult to follow. Of course, spiritual darkness cannot understand spiritual light, any more than moral degenerates can appreciate virtue (14b).

About three things Christ had no misgivings — *whence*, *here* and *whither*; the past, the present, and the future (14a).

Judgement should always be closely related to knowledge (15-18), and because the knowledge of the Pharisees was carnal, their judgement was cruel (15a). By '*I judge no man*,' Christ did not mean that he had no moral estimates (23,26), but that the day of judgement was not yet. If the testimony of two *men* be true, how can that testimony be challenged one of the bearers of which is God? (17,18).

Think carefully over verse 19. We know the Father only by knowing the Son. He who rejects the Son, rejects the Father also. Your relation to Jesus determines all your spiritual relations. Valuable teaching is in our portion on light, darkness, knowledge, ignorance, witness, discipleship, judgement, and providence; and all are involved in the relations which the Father, the Son, the world, and the soul sustain to one another.

Though the majority of Jesus' hearers did not at all understand what he meant, and the best of them only very partially, yet he poured out divinest revelation; he gave with both hands richly.

Thought: Truth is a home, not a house.

John 8:21-30

The self-revealer

This Gospel is not religious romance, as some imagine, but a faithful record of what John saw and heard. The Galilean fisherman could not have invented the ideas which constitute Christ's speeches here. Indeed at the time they were spoken he could scarcely have understood them; but two generations later, all was clear in the light of fulfilment.

Summarising the **discourse** in verses 21-59, Westcott says that it consists of two parts.
- The first part (21-30) contains the distinct presentation of the one object of faith with the declaration of the consequences of unbelief. This is closed by the notice of a large accession of disciples (30).
- The second part (31-58) gives an analysis of the essential character and issues of selfish belief and false Judaism. This is closed by the first open, violent assault upon the Lord (59).

Verse 22 is full of mockery. These Jews imagined that as Jesus was going where they could not go, he must be going to Gehenna by means of suicide. When speaking to such people as these, Jesus uses great plainness of speech; he says, '*Ye are from beneath,*' '*Ye are of this world,*' and three times, '*Ye shall die in your sins.*' They were on one side, and he on the other: *from above, not of this world.*

There was no confusion in Jesus' mind as to his origin, or as to his destiny; as to his eternal Sonship, or as to his present subordination to the Father. He knew that he was to be *lifted up* (28; 3:14; 12:32), not only to the cross, however, but also to the throne.

They should hesitate who criticise Christ's words, seeing that he attributes his teaching to the Father (26,28). Rationalistic criticism of Christ is a form of blasphemy. He spake and did always and only those things which pleased God. That is true of none other that ever lived. Do *you* believe on him (30)? What we think of Christ reveals our character, and determines our destiny.

Thought: The lifted-up will lift us up.

John 8:31-47

Plain speaking

This is a terrific utterance, wherein Jesus' lips and eyes send forth fire. He who could be very tender, could also be very terrible. Our passage treats of two things, *freedom* and *relationship*.

With reference to the former Jesus says that only by the truth can men be set free from the bondage of sin, that is, only by himself who is the truth (32,34,36). It is pathetic to hear enslaved people talking and singing about their freedom. '*Britons never shall be slaves.*' Oh! Scores of thousands are slaves to either drink, or lust, or greed, or pride, or selfishness, or to one or other of a thousand tyrants. These Jews imagined that they were free, but Jesus said that their father was the devil, and all his children are abject slaves.

'*Whosoever committeth sin is the servant of sin*' (34). Do you believe that? In a battle a soldier called out, 'I've caught a prisoner!' 'Bring him in,' replied an officer. 'He won't come,' said the soldier. 'Then come yourself,' replied the officer. 'He won't let me,' said the soldier. Question: *Who was the prisoner?* Every sinner is a slave, and every Christian is a free man. Only Christ's pierced hands can break your chains.

Then on the matter of *relationships*, Christ knows only two spiritual fatherships, God's and the devil's (38,44). In Christ's teaching there is no indefiniteness; all is as plain as words can make it. He thinks in terms of sharp antitheses, the historical and the spiritual, and external and the moral, the temporal and the eternal. These Jews were in the *natural* line of Abraham, but not in his *spiritual* line.

Children of Christian parents are not on that account Christians themselves. Only '*they which be of faith are blessed with faithful Abraham*' (Galatians 3:9). No one loves God who does not love Christ (42). What then about Jews, Muslims and Unitarians? It is because we are sinners that we do not love the sinless One (46).

Thought: There is liberty only in the Lord.

John 8:48-59

The eternal in time

Such a passage as this only shows that the unregenerate man, however religious he may be, is utterly incapable of understanding spiritual things. Here are people who made the claim that Jehovah was their God, yet they are saying that his Son is devil-possessed! Here are people who for ages have looked for salvation, and yet they are calling the Saviour a Samaritan! Here are people who boast that Abraham is their father, and yet they deny all that Abraham stood for! No one can honour the Father who dishonours the Son (49). Monotheism is not salvation. The devil is a monotheist (James 2:19), but he is not a Christian.

This is a day of shocking irreverence, and I will say this, that if what Jesus declares about himself in this chapter is not true, then, he is intellectually the most brilliant deceiver and the most cultured blasphemer the world has ever known. These are the only alternatives, so relate yourself to them quite definitely.

Jesus relates to one another *obedience and immortality* (51). If his teaching is not infallible and authoritative, why should we *keep* it; but if it is, then, why should we not? The *death* he refers to is not physical, but *spiritual*, but these sin-stupid Jews did not understand (51-53). '*Whom makest thou thyself?*' Surely he had made that plain enough! Abraham was very great, but Christ is incomparably greater (53,58).

> No Christian really dies:
> 'In vain they try
> To end my life, that can but end its woes.
> Is that a death-bed where a Christian lies?
> Yes! But not his; 'tis death itself there dies.'
> (Coleridge)

There are two ways in which people can be liars, either by not being what they profess to be, or by being what they declare they are not (55). Think of religious beings throwing stones at him who existed before Abraham was created (58,59)! Review and revere.

Thought: If we are not in Christ, Christ is not in us.

John 9:1-12

Light for darkness

This is a wonderful story, and not devoid of humour. Jesus sees people who do not see him, and he sees them that they may see him (1,7). They are all at sea who suppose that this man could not see because he had sinned before he came on the scene (2). The disciples wanted to *discuss* this man, but Jesus wanted to *deliver* him (3). Practical salvation is infinitely better than theological, philosophical, or psychological speculation. Let us concentrate upon the people's future rather than upon their past. Here was need, and what was wanted was help. Don't talk twaddle in the presence of trouble (2).

Verse 4 is a solemn and searching utterance. Mark *the urge to work*, *the kind of work*, *the time for work*, and *the end of work*. Do you feel this compulsion? How greatly the source of light is needed in this world of darkness (5)!

Verses 6,7, record a perplexing performance. We cannot tell why Jesus employed such means when he could have performed this miracle without the use of means at all, but we should occupy ourselves with the *what* of what he does, rather than with the *why*. What he tells us to do should at once be done. He who stops to ask *why*, may be left to whine.

I suppose that neighbourliness means interest in one another (8). Well, there is the man with both his eyes all right, and four verdicts are pronounced upon him: first, '*Is not this he?*'; second, '*This is he*'; third, '*He is like him*'; fourth, '*I am he.*'

Some people shut their mouth when they open their eyes; they are afraid to say that they see, that is, to confess Christ. Is that you? The people that had asked *who*? now ask *how*? and *where* (10,12)? It would be a good thing if all converts were catechised in this way; it would straighten them out. If you see, say so.

Thought: Christ was not a sight-seer, but a sight-giver.

John 9:13-25

Spiritual blindness

This man teaches us all a great lesson on *testimony*. Gather together all that he said in this talk, and you will see that his witness was simple and straightforward, and that *he kept to the facts*: the anointing, the command, the obedience and the result. He did not know who Jesus was; he did not know how the means effected such an end; nor was he versed in Judaistic casuistry; but *he did know that he could now see*, who all his life had been blind. Keep to the facts, tell what you know, and don't be tripped up by either critics or clowns.

The miracle was wrought on *the Sabbath* (16). Well, what better day on which to show mercy? If our religious institutions and conventions would prevent us doing good to anyone at any time, the sooner we modify or abandon such, the better. The Sabbath exists for the conscience, not for the calendar. The creed of these Pharisees was wooden, or they were (16a).

There was no room for wonder in their scheme of things. They lived in a world of small ideas, which was like a mud hut enclosing them. If they lifted a sheep from a hole on the Sabbath, they were saints; but he who gave sight on the Sabbath to one who had never seen, was a sinner! That's a crooked way of thinking.

But the question of this man's identity is not settled yet (18). It is good when one is so completely changed by the grace of God that his identity is called into question. And now enter the parents (18-23), and a miserable couple they are. I pity the children of cowards. The mother ought to have gone frantic with delight, but, instead, she played the craven and missed her chance.

What were they afraid of? Ex-communication (22). Well, what of that? Better be outside the church with Christ, than inside without him. It is not ecclesiastical courts that we should fear, but everlasting condemnation.

Thought: Be a preacher, not a poltroon.

John 9:26-41

Full illumination

We are now to witness the last scene in this drama, in which tragedy and comedy so strangely mingle. Who? What? When? Why? Where? rattled from these critics as from a machine gun, and answered, or unanswered, the fact remained: a man, blind all his life, who now can see; can see for the first time his craven parents, and these blind leaders of the people.

But he stuck to the facts (25). He was not a philosopher, but a witness, not a theologian, but a convert. I would like to see a man like this turned loose in many of our divinity halls. He would know nothing about hexateucal criticism, or the synoptic problem, but he would glow with a new-found joy, and with rugged eloquence tell that Christ had saved him. In vain would professor or student ask for his theory of the atonement or of biblical inspiration; his only answer would be,

> 'E'er since by faith I saw the stream
> His flowing wounds supply,
> Redeeming love has been my theme,
> And shall be till I die.'

One truly converted soul is worth all the apologetics that were ever written. The Christian witness is not on the bookshelf, but in the renewed life; it is not a matter of logic, but of love.

But, of course, one who is out and out will have to pay for his profession, and not so much at the hands of the ungodly as of the professor of religion (28,34). It is always easier to revile than to reason; to clear people out, than to convince them.

But when they cast him out, Jesus found him out. Losing the synagogue, he won the Saviour. To the blessing of natural sight, was now added the grace of spiritual sight (35-38). At the beginning of this chapter a *man* is blind, but at the end, a *nation* (39-41). Can *you* see?

Thought: Eye-balls are no good without eye-sight.

John 10:1-18

A pastoral portion

This passage arises immediately out of the previous chapter. The religious leaders there were hirelings and not true shepherds; they drove one sheep away (9:34), but the true shepherd found him. The key to the present discourse is verse 16 RV, which speaks of the *fold* and the *flock* (Greek: *aulê*, and *poimnê*). In relation to the *fold*, Christ is the *door* (7-10), and in relation to the *flock*, he is the *shepherd* (11-16). First, we have *the parable* (1-5), and then *the interpretation and application* of it (6-18).

The parable (1-5). Consider the *sheepfold*, the *door*, the *sheep*, the *thief*, the *porter*, the *stranger*, and the *shepherd*. Part of this Jesus interprets. The thieves and robbers are all false messiahs and self-commissioned teachers who preceded Jesus. The sheep are true believers, and Christ himself is both the door into the fold and the Shepherd of the sheep. As to the rest, the sheepfold is the true church; the strangers are unqualified shepherds, and should be distinguished from the thieves and robbers; and the porter is 'the Spirit acting through his appointed ministers'. The people to whom Jesus spoke did not understand, but that is no reason why we should not.

The interpretation and application (6-18). Study carefully the **door** paragraph (7-10). The sinner who would become a Christian must enter into Christ by Christ and must find Christ to be the scope of his life, and his support. Thus, as Westcott says, 'The fullness of the Christian life is exhibited in its three elements—safety, liberty, support' (9). Christ designs for his people not only life, but abounding life (10). Is it yours?

Study now this **shepherd** paragraph (11-16). Christ is the Good Shepherd in regard of his *devotion* (11-13), and of his *sympathy* (14-16). Christ plainly teaches, both before the cross and after it, that his death was voluntary (17,18; Revelation 1:18, *'became dead'*).

Thought: Are you a sheep or a goat?

John 10:19-30

Eternal life

The main thought of the previous passage continues throughout this one (cf. verses 4,24). Christ has always been a dividing factor among men (9:16; 10:19). The alternatives here are devil or divine (20,21). Mad or Messiah. Well, demons won't heal, and lunatics cannot, but Jesus did (21). That should have given the Jews something to think about.

The Feast of Dedication was held about the middle of December for a week (22). It was established by Judas Maccabaeus, 165 BC, to commemorate the purification of the Temple from the pollutions of Antiochus, and its re-dedication to the service of Jehovah.

Being winter (22), Jesus taught in a sheltered place (23). The Jews would hold Jesus responsible for their suspense (24), but it was occasioned by their want of spiritual discernment (25), and this was due to a want of vital relationship with Christ by faith (26).

Here the figure of the parable is taken up again. *Eternal life* cannot be secured by labouring or suffering, but may be received by faith as God's free gift (28). *Eternal* tells not of the duration of the life, but of its quality. They who have it not, *cause themselves to perish* (28). The sinner is always self-destroyed. Omit *man* in verse 28, then the thought includes all foes temporal and spiritual; neither men nor demons can sever the saved from the Saviour. See Romans 8:35-39.

The Christian can fall *in* the way, but not *out* of it. A son may disgrace his father, but he can never cease to be his father's son. This truth allows us room for presumption, but supplies every motive for perseverance. Omit *man* in verse 29 also. They who are in the shepherd's fold are in the Father's hand. Verse 30 is against Unitarianism.

Thought: Are you hidden in God's hand?

John 10:31-42

Rejected evidence

Stones prove nothing (31,32). They are the artillery of cads. I wonder if these Jews felt the biting irony of Jesus' reply (32)! It is bad enough to be spiritually blind, but proudly to advertise it is pitiable (33). These people were Arians before Arius, but they had a greater than Athanasius to deal with them. Jesus appeals *to the Scriptures* which they professed to believe (34,35), *to his claim for himself* (36), and *to his works* (37,38). There was therefore no lack of evidence; but, given a certain state of mind and heart, evidence is of no use. Someone has said that a bigot is like the pupil of the eye, the more light you pour on to it, the more it contracts.

It was the man who was claiming to be God (36). In Christ two natures dwelt in the union of one personality, and in these records sometimes the one is prominent, and sometimes the other. Those who will not repose faith in Christ's *person*, are asked to accept the witness of his *works* (38). That is fair. What about it? Look at the dominating purpose of this Gospel (20:31) and then read this chapter again. The phrase, '*he went forth out of*', occurs here only (39, RV).

Jesus now retreats to Perea (40), and his ministry draws to a close where it had begun (1:28). He retired to a scene of blessed memories, that he might refresh himself and be quiet after all that had happened. '*Beyond Jordan*' was where he was baptised, where he first heard the testimony of John, where he found his first disciples.

Such places we all need at times. It does not do to dwell for ever in the city; we need the quiet of the mountain, the comfort of the river, and the shelter of the forest. You can be a blessing to others there (42). John was not a wonderworker, but a witness.

Thought: He who is the first and the last, should be loved from the first to the last.

John 11:1-16

The death of Lazarus

The *raising of Lazarus* is the seventh and last sign recorded by this evangelist, which Jesus wrought before the cross. These seven form a significant whole, and are selected from the thirty-six miracles which Jesus wrought in keeping with the purpose of this record.

It may well be asked why the Synoptists did not record so great an event as the raising of Lazarus. I think you will find the answer in 12:10,11. Assuming that the three first Gospels were written before AD 70, to have broadcast this event would have been to imperil the life of Lazarus, but when John wrote around AD 95, almost certainly Lazarus was dead again, so that this record would do him no harm.

The story is in four main parts: 1. **Jesus and the disciples** (1-16). 2. **Jesus and the sisters** (17-32). 3. **Jesus and Lazarus** (33-44). 4. **Jesus and the Jews** (45-57).

This passage is in two sections.

- *Reception of the news about Lazarus* (1-6).

The family at Bethany is given no small place in the gospel story, for they were among Jesus' most intimate friends (1,2,5). If he received comfort from them, they derived great honour from him.

In this first section (1-6) two things must impress us; first, that Jesus said the sickness was '*not unto death*', yet, Lazarus died; and second, that when the news came of the family's trouble, Jesus tarried where he was for another two days. These two points are vitally related. First, Jesus had resolved to raise Lazarus; second, in order to do so, he gave him time to die.

- *Decision to go to Bethany* (7-16).

In the second section (7-16) mark the *fear* (8) and *dullness* (16) of the disciples, and Jesus' consciousness of *vocation* (9,10), and of *power* (11,15). Where Christ is loved, *death* is *sleep* (14,11).

Thought: Christ's delays are not denials.

John 11:17-31

The two sisters

The first part of the story showed us Jesus and the disciples (1-16); this one shows us **Jesus and the sisters** (17-32). This view of Martha and Mary should be studied with that given in Luke 10:38-42. Together these furnish a most instructive psychological study.

These sisters were quite different, but both good; both facts being brought out by both evangelists. Martha was active, but Mary was contemplative. When Martha *went*, Mary *sat* (20). Be sure not to draw from this the inference that Mary loved Jesus less than Martha, or that Martha loved Lazarus more than Mary.

Martha

Martha's nimbleness of mind is reflected in the words '*if . . . but* (21,22). She does not say, '*If thou hadst come at once*', for she is not complaining, but she is expressing her profound faith in the love and power of her friend. Notwithstanding, her faith was only in part enlightened, for she spoke of Christ praying as he never speaks of himself, using the word *aiteo*, of an inferior to a superior, instead of *erotao*, of equals (22).

Furthermore, her faith was for the future, not the present (23,24); but when Jesus revealed himself to her at the resurrection (25,26), her faith immediately responded (27). Blessed indeed is it when revelation is so apprehended.

This confession of Martha's must stand beside Peter's (6:69).

Mary

The other sister now comes into view (28-32). Jesus had asked for her (28), and when she heard this, she sat no longer (29). Contemplative people can move quickly when occasion requires. The reason for the secret message was that Jesus wished to meet Mary alone, without the Jews. How considerate the Master is! Bereavement is no occasion for vulgar curiosity. This is a tender and beautiful story.

Thought: You increase the faith you exercise.

John 11:32-46

Life from the dead

The third division of this chapter is **Jesus and Lazarus** (33-44). Here is a deeply impressive passage on *the emotions of Jesus*. We are told that, in the presence of this death, '*he groaned . . . was troubled . . . wept . . . again groaning*' (33-38). Both as man, and as God, Jesus suffered. Pity, sympathy, love and grief all expressed themselves in groans and tears.

We never read that Jesus laughed, but we are not to infer that he never did so, but he came to a world of sin, and came to deal with it; hence the gravity which characterised him. Surely his *trouble* at this time (33) arose from the significance of death as the fruit of sin, and from the consciousness of his own approaching passion.

The two miracles, around which, in one view, this record moves in an elipse, are *the healing of the blind man* and *the raising of Lazarus* (37). '*Could he not?*' Oh, yes, but Jesus did not do all that he could. He always did the better thing that people might have the bigger blessing. The death of Lazarus proved to be gain, not loss. At first the sisters felt only the thorn; afterward they saw the rose. Compare Martha's two utterances, verses 27 and 39. What contradictions we are!

Compare 40 with 4. Jesus did not do what they could do for themselves. They could not raise the dead, so he did that (43,44), but they could remove the stone, so he did not do that (41). He will do wonderful things for us if only we will remove the stones. An angel removed it from Jesus' grave, because it was too heavy for the women. How kind God is!

Not many of Jesus' prayers are recorded. Collect and study them. Here is one (41,42). He had spoken to the Father about raising Lazarus. He spoke to him about everything he did. Do you? The Lord's voice was heard in Hades (43).

Ponder verse 44. Marvellous! The first was the blessing of *life*, the second, of *liberty*. Have you both?

Thought: All who come forth should go forth.

John 11:47-57

A priest prophesies

The fourth part of this story tells of **Jesus and the Jews** (45-57). Already we have had occasion to observe what opposite effects the same act or word may have on people. See it here (45,46). All through the record *belief* and *unbelief* lie side by side, and develop in parallel lines (cf.9:16; 10:20,21).

What effect has the gospel had upon you? It is a good thing when religious complacency and smug satisfaction are disturbed; when moral and spiritual enervation are aroused by the incoming of vigorous air. This is what happened here (47,48). '*What do we . . . for this man doeth?*' That question may well be put from the opposite side today—'What do we Christians do . . . for the world, the flesh, and the devil do?'

But the anxiety of the Sanhedrin was not motivated by any spiritual concern, but by a sense of insecurity which they had begun to feel regarding themselves (48). In the reply which Caiaphas made, there is a note of contempt for those to whom he speaks: '*Ye know nothing at all.*'

Then follows a word which was more far-reaching than the speaker knew (50-52). 'In virtue of his office he so utters his own thoughts as to pronounce a sentence of God unconsciously.' Unwittingly he interprets the results of the death of Christ truly, and so his utterance was '*not of himself*'. But could an unsaved man speak prophetically? Yes, Balaam did. He who once used the mouth of an ass has often used the mouth of unbelievers. Ponder over that phrase—'*the children of God*' (52). It savours more of the epistles than of the Gospels.

Consider to what extent Christ's attitude to you is affected by your attitude towards him (53,54).

These people purified themselves for the Passover (55). Do you prepare yourself for the Lord's Table? Read 1 Corinthians 11:26-32.

Thought: Each of us is either a friend or a foe of Christ: which?

John 12:1-19

The guest and the King

Westcott divides the fifty verses of this chapter as follows: The Lord's relation *to his disciples* (1-11), *to the multitude* (12-19), and *to the larger world outside* (20-36a), followed by two summary judgements on the whole issue of Christ's works: the judgement *of the evangelist* (36b-43), and *of the Lord himself* (44-50). With this chapter, the public ministry of Christ closes.

By consulting a *Harmony of the Gospels* you will see what John omits which the Synoptists include, and what he records which they omit. Such a study is profoundly impressive and instructive. John's Gospel begins and ends with a sacred week (cf. verse 1, with chapter 1:29,35,43 and 2:1).

There begins here what we call the *Passion Week*. On the **Friday** Jesus and his disciples arrived before 6.0 p.m., from Jericho, and at the home at Bethany. It would appear that this supper (2) took place on the **Saturday**, after 6.0 p.m., the close of the Sabbath.

This anointing by Mary should be compared with the incident recorded in Luke 7:36-38, and we shall see how equal devotion can be expressed in different ways. The fragrance of Mary's ointment has filled more than the house in which Jesus was, and also the grunt of Judas has been heard further afield (3-5). Verse 6 is the comment of the evangelist on this incident, after a lapse of over sixty years. All motives will be revealed some day.

'*The next day*' (12) refers to **Sunday**, which we call Palm Sunday. Jesus' triumphal entry into Jerusalem was in fulfilment of prophecy (Zechariah 9). What course would history have taken had the Jews then received him as their messianic king? Verse 16 is also a reflection of the evangelist (cf. verse 6). The dilemma of the Pharisees is becoming more acute (19, cf.11:47,48). Compare '*if we let him alone*', with '*let her alone*' (11:48;12:7).

Thought: You cannot give Christ anything too costly.

John 12:20-36

A temptation resisted

Some harmonists place this visit of the Greeks on Monday, but more generally it is thought to have been on Tuesday, at the close of the great controversy. If this latter be the case, then John makes no reference to the events of the Monday. John records a controversy which the Synoptists omit (chapters 5 to 10), and he omits a controversy which they record (Matthew 21:23—23:39).

If the visit of the Greeks be read after the Matthew record just referred to, the reason for their approach will be clear. Jesus' own people had rejected him, and without doubt, they intimated their willingness to receive him if he would go to their nation.

The passage contains the *request* (20-22), the *reply* (23-33), and the *warning* (34-36a). The request is not recorded, but must be inferred from the reply. It evidently was a pleasing proposition, but one that Jesus could not consider. Two passages in the reply make this clear. First, *the principle of service* which Christ enunciated (23-25): usefulness by unselfishness; sovereignty by sacrifice. And second, *the prayer of Christ* (27,28a). '*What shall I say? "Father, save me from this hour?" But for this cause came I unto this hour.* (No, I will say) *"Father, glorify thy name."*'

Following this, came the declaration of the Father (28), referring back to the baptism, and the transfiguration (Matthew 3:17; and 17:5), and on the cross (verses 23,32). Alas, that still the voice of God is to many no more than a rumble (29)!

To Jesus that hour was *critical* (31, Greek). In verse 32 the *fact, manner*, and *effect* of Christ's death are declared. He who was about to lay down his life was the light in which men were in danger of not walking (34-36a). John has much (in his epistles) to say about walking in the light. Yes, Christ does abide for ever, but not as the corn does which is not sown (34,24).

Thought: The secret of life is death.

John 12:37-50

The success of apparent failure

Our passage is in two distinct parts. In verses 37-43, John connects the apparent failure of the Lord's work with the prophetic teaching of Isaiah, quoting from chapters 6 and 53.

Take time to be impressed by these predictions of seeming failure. So far as worthy results were concerned, neither Isaiah, Jeremiah, nor Ezekiel was given any encouragement; each was allotted a hard and thankless task; but the reward of their labours came from other hands. So was it with Jesus. '*Though he had done so many miracles before them, yet they believed not on him*' (37). Then had he failed? Oh, no. Some apparent successes are consummate failures, and some seeming failures are great successes. It would be a serious thing for most Christian workers if they were to be judged by the visible results of their labours.

Observe, John identifies the divine person which Isaiah saw in his vision with Christ (41). Study the *Christophanies* of the Old Testament.

What follows shows that no labour for God is in vain; there always will be some who are won (42), though, too often, even these are very disappointing (42,43). Is there anything which you love *more than the praise of God*?

In the second paragraph (44-50) our Lord summarises his teaching, speaking first of *his person* (44-46), and then of *his words* (47-50). Jesus makes plain here what is evident throughout the whole record, that there are but two attitudes, one or other of which each of us must assume towards Christ: that of belief, or of unbelief. In consequence there are but two results, one or other of which will fall to each of us: salvation or condemnation. '*The last day*' (48) will pronounce on all our days.

Remember, Christ's authority was of divine origin, and therefore infallible and final. There is no court of appeal beyond him. What is his verdict on you?

Thought: Christ is the critic. Let us covet his commendation.

John 13:1-17

At a supper

With chapter 12 ends the first great division of this Gospel—**the revelation of God to the world as life** (1:19 to 12:50). With chapter 13 begins the second great division—**the revelation of God to the disciples as light** (13:1 to 17:26). Then follows the last division—**the revelation of God to the disciples and the world as love** (18:1 to 20:31). The first part represents the *outer court* of the Tabernacles, the second, the *Holy Place*, and the third, the *Holiest of All*. The furniture which dominates in these parts respectively is—the *brazen altar*; the *table of shewbread, altar of incense* and *golden candlestick*; and the *ark* and *mercy-seat*. This Gospel is full of Tabernacle symbolism.

Chapters 13 to 17 are peculiar to John, and they are inestimably precious. Observe how our passage is introduced. At least eight statements of great importance lead up to what is said in verse 4. Write them down one beneath the other, and ponder them. In whose house was the Passover observed?

Distinguish between this feet-washing and that of Luke 7:44. The latter was a regulation, but the former was a revelation, first in *deed* (4-11), and then, in *word* (12-20). Christ's actions were parables, and his messages were miracles.

Mark the part which Peter played on this occasion (6,8,9), and Jesus' replies (7,8,10,11), especially verse 10; 'He that is *bathed* needeth not save to *wash* his feet' (Greek). The Master plainly declares here that all the apostles, except Judas, were converted men. There is no *spiritual washing* for anyone who has not been entirely *bathed* in the crimson flood.

How imperative is *ought* in verse 14: compare 1 John 2:6; 3:16; 4:11. Measure your life by that rod. These men, and all Christians, are related to Christ as *learners* and *servants*, corresponding to *Lord* and *Master* in verse 14.

Thought: The father of happiness is knowledge, and her mother is action.

John 13:18-30

The traitor retires

In paragraph verses 4-20 we are in the *sunlight of selflessness*, but in verses 21-30 we are in the *shadow of selfishness*. The one part tells of the tenderness of Jesus, and the other part, of the treachery of Judas. There is no cup without its bitter drop, no rose without a thorn, no sky without a cloud, no song without a sigh. A picture without any shadow is not like anything in nature. Hard by Jesus was Judas. Were heaven and hell ever nearer to one another?

That Jesus lived in the company of Judas for two years, knowing what he was and would do, must be regarded as a moral miracle. That the other apostles never suspected Judas must be put down, either to their want of perception, or to his refined hypocrisy. But truth comes out at last; sooner or later the good and the bad must be separated. Have you any *doubt* about betrayal? (22). Are you quite sure that you are in no degree guilty? Think.

John refers more than once to Jesus' being in *trouble* (21, cf. 11:33; 12:27). Great as were his physical pains, they cannot be compared with his spiritual sufferings. The sin of Judas shocked him to the bottom of his soul. The only mention of Satan in his Gospel is here (27).

The words in verses 24-26 were spoken secretly, but those in verse 27, openly; cf. verses 28,29. Judas never partook of the Lord's Supper, but from verse 29 it would appear that neither did he partake of the Passover. All that is recorded in this division (chapters 12 to 17) occurred on the Thursday night of Passion Week.

There are degrees of disloyalty to Christ. Thomas doubted, Peter denied, but Judas delivered him to death. In verse 27, Jesus did not help Judas to form his resolve, he simply told him to accomplish quickly what he had already determined to do. What can you make of Judas?

Thought: Love is loyalty's truest safeguard.

John 13:31-38

Intimation of departure

Up to now we have been considering what Jesus *did* for his disciples (1-30). Now, we are to consider what he *said* to them. The *discourse* which follows (13:31 to 16:33) divides into two parts: that which was spoken *in the upper room* (13:31 to 14:31), and that which was spoken *on the way to Gethsemane* (15:1 to 16:33).

In the first of these, the disciples ask, and Jesus answers questions. Hear *Peter* (36), and *Thomas* (14:5), and *Philip* (14:8), and *Jude* (14:22).

This passage is dominated by the idea of the approaching *separation. Now* in verse 31, is most significant. 'It expresses at once the feeling of deliverance from the traitor's presence and his free acceptance of the issues of the traitor's work.' Jesus here relates himself not as the eternal Son to the Father, but as the Son of Man to God (31).

Five times in two verses he speaks of *glory*. He saw the throne (31,32). He tells the disciples of his coming departure (33), and says by what the world would recognise his people after he had gone (34,35). The ideal he sets before them is that they should relate themselves to one another as he had related himself to them, in love.

At this point **Peter** opens the series of questions which follow. He asks *whither?* and *why?* Peter was a type of man that one instinctively likes. He was impulsive, erratic, and, in a way, ambitious, but at heart he was true. He had not learned the extent of his weakness, nor did he remotely imagine that he was on the edge of a precipice. That there were slumbering loyalties in this man his later life proves, but at this time he was not under the only true control. He came under that at Pentecost; then was fulfilled chapter 1:42.

Thought: Don't skate on thin ice.

John 14:1-14

An apocalypse of the Father

In this passage Christ reveals *the Father and his own relation to him*. In these few verses he names the Father twelve times. Summarise his teaching on this subject. In the first paragraph Jesus says *where* he is going, and *why*. He is going to the Father's house, and he is going to prepare a place for his people. He further says that he himself is the way to the goal which he sets before his disciples.

It is he who was sore troubled (13:21) who exhorts us not to be troubled (1). His troubles were saving, but ours are often sinful.

In verse 3, read, '*I come again, and will receive.*' The coming is not an isolated act, such as the second advent, but his coming in its progressive and eternal reality (cf. verses 18,23,28). What we speak of as the second advent is the last stage in the fulfilment of this wonderful promise.

Thomas asks a question about the *way*, and draws from Jesus the great declaration of verse 6. What a *truth* is this: that Christ is the entrance to the way, is the way itself, and is the end of the way. He says, '*I am*' — not merely, 'I open,' or 'I reveal.' *Way, truth*, and *life* are personal.

If possible, verse 7 is still more amazing. Here are *distinction* and *identity*; Christ is absolutely one with the Father, so that to have seen him is to have seen the Father; and yet he is the Son and not the Father.

Now, **Philip** has a request to make which arises immediately out of verse 7. Had Philip understood what Jesus had said, the request would never have been made. Jesus can only repeat with emphasis what he had already said (9). No one can know God as Father except through the redeeming Christ. Natural religion has nothing to say to us about the Father, neither has Judaism, but Christianity only. This knowledge is reached by faith. *Believest*, in verse 10, is singular; in verse 11 it is plural, all the disciples being addressed.

Thought: Revelation requires apprehension.

John 14:15-31

The advent and work of the Spirit

Now follows the remainder of the conversation *in the house*. Christ declares that the proof of love for him is obedience (15). That combination of moral qualities is unique. Consider the matter. He then plainly announces the advent of the Spirit. The promise was fulfilled on the day of Pentecost. Mark the Trinity in verse 16: *I, the Father, another Comforter*. The promise is that the *accompanying* Spirit would shortly become the *indwelling* Spirit (17b). All that is mystery to the world, which lacks the discerning faculty. When the Spirit came, Christ came in a new way (18).

There is progress in Christ's teaching on the subject of identification. First, there is identification of *Father* and *Son* in verses 7,9-11, then of the *Spirit* with them (16), and now of *all believers* with the Trinity (20). The relation of love and obedience is again brought to notice (21), and how richly is obeying love rewarded!

Peter, Thomas, and Philip have spoken; now **Jude** asks a question (22). It arises out of what Jesus had said in verse 19. The answer may be summarised in this way. The Father reveals himself only to the obedient. Only they who love him are obedient. The world does not love him, therefore does not obey him, and so he does not manifest himself unto the world (23,24).

Christ could teach the disciples only so much because of their very limited spiritual understanding, but when their capacity was enlarged they would be taught more. Compare *these things* (25) with *all things* (26), Christ's work, and the Spirit's.

Glory, love, peace, joy—these are the words which Christ rings out in the shadow of the cross. He only was calm in the midst of confusion, because he was sure of the Father. Divine revelation has always had the future in mind (25,29). '*Let us go hence.*' He never sends us alone.

Thought: Peace and worry cannot dwell in the same heart.

John 15:1-17

Fruitfulness and friendship

If verses 1-10 can be called a parable, it is the only parable in this Gospel, and one not recorded by the other evangelists. This is noteworthy, seeing that Jesus taught so much by parables, and must be accounted for by the purpose of the Gospel, and in view of those for whom it was written—not Hebrews, *Matthew*; nor Romans, *Mark*; nor Greeks, *Luke*; but Christians.

We learn from 14:31, that Christ and his disciples left the upper room; probably they walked across to the Temple, and the golden vine on the gates would suggest this great lesson on *the Christian's vital union with his Lord* (1-10). Distinguish the *husbandman*, the *vine*, and the *branches*: the Father, Christ and his church viewed together, and every separate believer. We shall misunderstand this parable unless we recognise that it embraces all Christian profession, whether real or not, as does the parable of the virgins. Only so can we understand verse 6.

Another thing must be distinguished, namely, our relation to Christ on the ground of sovereign grace, and our experience of him depending on our soul's attitude. All Christians are, as we say, converted, but all are not consecrated. Our passage is an exhortation to consecration and ever greater fruitfulness.

Every Christian is in the vine, but every Christian is not a friend of Christ's. This is the subject of verses 11-17. *This friendship is based on obedience* (14), and carries with it special privileges (15). Another lesson taught is that the friends of Christ have a special fellowship with one another (12,13).

The whole passage has much to teach us on the subjects of *fruitfulness, chastisement, dependence, abiding, prayer, discipleship, obedience, love, joy, sacrifice, election*, and *perseverance*. These discourses are the profoundest teaching which Jesus gave on earth.

Thought: Our spiritual state should be congruous with our spiritual standing in Christ.

John 15:18-27

The church and the world

The subject of **Christ, the Christian, and the world**, follows logically from what has been said already. Some good people talk of, and work for, a spiritualised world. They would be more in harmony with the teaching of Christ if they recognised the danger of a carnalised church. The world can never be spiritualised. It is in nature essentially opposed to Christianity, and in principle hates it (18). Worldly love is one thing, and Christian love is another, and these loves can never love one another (19).

No Christian can, with any hope of success, *go into the world* (Matthew 28:19), until he has *come out of it* (19): service here is conditioned on separation. The Christian who is loved by the world which hates his Lord has good reason for alarm (20). Righteousness and unrighteousness are irreconcilable principles; they stand for ever opposed, and the church and Christian stand only and always to lose by compromise. This attitude of the world to Christ is inexcusable, for he has wrought and taught in its midst; it cannot therefore plead ignorance (22-25).

I have heard people talk about *London for Christ, New York for Christ*, and so on. Our passage makes such a slogan not only worthless but perilous, for it promotes the misdirection of valuable energies. Change it to *Christ for London*, etc., and we have his own ambition and warrant. Our business is to bear witness to him with and by the Holy Spirit (26,27).

The great need of today is that the church recover her lost vision, that she recognise the terms of her calling, and that she stand uncompromisingly towards the world, the flesh, and the devil. *'The servant is not greater than his Lord'* (20). If you are in worldly favour, sit down and think.

Thought: To abide in Christ we must abandon the world.

John 16:1-15

The mission of the Spirit

In this chapter Christ has much to say about the Holy Spirit, relative to the world in 1-11, and to the disciples in 12-15. **The Holy Spirit and the world** (1-11). Throughout the centuries the world has revealed its attitude towards Christ by persecution of his people. This has expressed itself in various ways, at different times: sometimes viciously, and sometimes politely; sometimes by calculated cruelty, and sometimes by cynical indifference; but the same spirit motivates every form of opposition.

Persecution of Christians has come from opposite quarters, as, for example, the fanaticism of the Roman church on the one hand, and the atheism of Soviet Russia on the other hand, but ignorance of God and of Christ is chargeable against both (1-4a).

But Christians have not been left to themselves in the day of their need. The grievous departure was followed by a gladsome arrival (4b-7). The visible gave place to the invisible, and the local made room for the universal. A seeming disaster was, in reality, a great provision; and the Spirit in the church now addresses the world as Christ in the flesh never could have done (8-11).

The text, verse 8, is analysed in verses 9-11. The categories of *sin, righteousness*, and *judgement*, include all that is essential in the determination of the religious state of man, and to these the work of the Paraclete is referred. These three categories call attention to *man* (9), *Christ* (10), the *devil* (11): to man's condition as sinful (9), and then, to the alternatives that lie before him: *righteousness* to be obtained from without (10), or *judgement* to be borne (11).

The Holy Spirit and the disciples (12-15). In verses 12-15 is revealed the Spirit's work for the church through the apostles. The *Gospel records* are in view in 14:26; the *Acts* and *Epistles* in verse 13a, and the *Revelation* in 13b. Mark the Trinity in verse 15.

Thought: Only the convicted can be instructed.

John 16:16-33

Goodbye

The profoundest of all Jesus' discourses is now drawing to a close. He has spoken to this little company of many things, the full meaning of which they could not then appreciate (14:29). But at the end of the first century all is now clear to the apostle John. But these words are exhaustless; no one has extracted from them all the nourishment which they contain.

In conclusion, the Master speaks to his disciples words of comfort and cheer. A great change is about to take place, and they are prepared for it by what is said in verses 16-22. *Jesus is going, but he will come again* (16).

That puzzled these men (17,18), but Jesus went on to tell them of the *death* which would plunge them into aching sorrow, and of the *resurrection* which would lift them into rapturous joy (19,20). He illustrates this (21), and then reaffirms that their joy will come out of their sorrow; the cause of the one shall prove the cause of the other (22). There is a Christian doctrine of *sorrow* and *joy* of which the world knows nothing.

Next, Jesus speaks of his disciples' future intercourse with him (23-30). After the great change, how is fellowship to be maintained? Jesus tells them that the familiar intercourse is not to be terminated, but transmuted.

Read verses 19 and 23 together. The disciples were constantly asking Jesus questions, but henceforth there would be no need so to do. In the Greek two words are used for *ask* in verse 23; first *erótésete*, then, *aitéséte*. Through the glorified Christ we now may come directly to the Father.

Mark the connection between *prayer* and *joy* (24). The above two words occur again in verse 26: *Ask* is *aiteó*, and *pray* is *erótaó*, this latter being used in this Gospel only of Christ's prayers. In the closing words Christ bids his disciples and us all to *cheer up*. Though *in the world*, the greater truth is that we are *in him* (33).

Thought: As sinners we must come over before as saints we can overcome.

John 17:1-12

The Saviour prays

Here discourse to men passes into converse with God, and the *prayer* is the consummation and ratification of the *teaching*. Bengel says, 'In this prayer Christ embraces all that from chapter 13:31 he has said, and sets his seal to all things already done, looking to things past, present, and future. It is a tacit intimation of the new Pentecost at hand. In all the Scripture this chapter is in words most easy, in their meanings most profound.'

We may distinguish three parts in this prayer, though the theme throughout is one. Look at these.

● **Christ and his Father** (1-5). Connect verses 1-5 with chapter 1:1-5. In no plainer words could claim to deity be made. *Father, Son, eternal life to know Christ, glory with the Father before the world was*—these words take us deeply into the God-consciousness of Christ. Neither John nor anyone else could ever have conceived such ideas; these are reported utterances, and they come to us warm with the breath of the intercessor. While accomplishing his earthly task Jesus lived in profoundest intimacy with his Father (4). No disciple will finish his work who neglects prayer.

● **Christ and his apostles** (6-19). After this, Christ's thought turns to his apostles. How tender are the words, '*The men which thou gavest me out of the world*' (6). This was not all the fruit of his labour, but it was the best of it. They had not always understood, but light was breaking (7,8). He was about to leave his apostles, but he would not forget them (9). They were in an indissoluble bond of life with the Father and the Son (10), and so he prays for their keeping (11).

We cannot be kept unless we are saved, but we may be saved without being kept. Remember that Christ is praying today that you may be kept today. Help him to answer that prayer (Jude 21). Christ's standpoint in this prayer is *heaven* (12).

Thought: I need not sin while Christ prays.

John 17:13-26

The Saviour's prayer

In verses 6-19 Christ is *praying for his apostles*. Christ's mind turns from the past (12) to the future (13). In verse 12 he says, '*While I was . . . in the world*', now he says, '*These things I speak in the world*' (13): *there* in spirit, but *here* in presence. The prayer was uttered aloud that the disciples might draw strength from the words which they heard (13).

But the *joy* which he wills for them must be won through conflict (14,15). These verses recall what he had said in 15:18-25. The Christian life is a struggle, not a reverie; a battle, not a dream. Don't pray to be taken out of it all to heaven, but that you may be kept true while you are here (15). It is the easiest but not the noblest thing to quit the field.

Small words are apt to be overlooked but pay attention to *even as* in verse 16, and *even so* in verse 18. Try and imagine the significance of these comparisons. The believer as detached from the world as the Saviour himself! And placed on the same level of calling and service as he! For such work we need the character and power which can come only by *sanctification in the truth*, which is the sum of the Christian revelation (17).

● **Christ and his church** (20-26). Having prayed for himself (1-5), and for his apostles (6-19), Jesus now prays for his church (20-26). What boundless hope there is in verse 20. In those eleven men Christ saw the '*great multitude which no man can number*'; in those few seeds he saw the harvest waving gold over all the earth.

He says that the conviction of the world will be by the unity of the church (21). Then can we wonder that the world is not convicted? Here is another *even as*. Wonderful! But remember, unity is not uniformity, neither is it external union. The reunion of Christendom would be the greatest religious disaster of the ages. Experimental Christian unity is based on *knowledge* and *love* (24-26). Are you helping to answer this prayer?

Thought: Vital Christianity is oneness with Christ.

John 18:1-14

The deadly deed

With this chapter begins the last main division of this Gospel — **the revelation of God to the disciples and the world as love** (18:1 to 20:31). *Divine life* dominates the first (chapters 1 to 12), *divine light*, the second (chapters 13 to 17), and *divine love* the third (chapters 18 to 20). Together these make a perfect revelation of God in Christ. Without the last, the other two would be not only enigmatic but impossible, for only by the *love* that made the supreme sacrifice can *life* and *light* come to men; therefore this third division of the Gospel is not supplemental but fundamental.

The betrayal (1-11). Our first paragraph records the betrayal. Mark the place (1,2). Gethsemane was familiar to Jesus and his disciples, both as a place of fellowship and of rest. Now follows the arrest (3-9). In any view, what a farce this was! Two hundred soldiers from the garrison, and a large posse of police, 'with lanterns and torches and weapons', to arrest one man, at dead of night, when no one was about to interfere with them!

Compare their panic with Jesus' peace, their devilry with his divinity, and their impotence with his power. Jesus submitted, not because he had to, but because he chose to (4,8,11), in fulfilment of a divine commission and mission, of which he was fully conscious, and to which he was wholly consecrated (4,9,11).

We learn from Philippians 2:6-8 that he lays aside his glory, but here a flash of it strikes fear into this crowd, and lays some of them low (6).

Peter, as usual, acts from untutored impulse (10), but his Master was not helped by that (11). How much of our intended help is in fact a hindrance, because offered in the energy of the flesh instead of in the power of the Spirit!

The trials. After the betrayal come the trials (18:12 to 19:16), the first *ecclesiastical* (18:12-27), and the second *civil* (18:28 to 19:16). Distinguish carefully the six stages of the trial of Jesus, by a comparison of the four Gospels.

Thought: Prepare for coming crises.

John 18:15-27

Two trials

● **The trial of Jesus** (12-14, 19-24). The three stages of the *ecclesiastical* trial were, *before Annas* (13), *before Caiaphas* (24) and *before the Sanhedrin*—this last not being mentioned by John. In this passage two trials are taking place at the same time, one of *Jesus* and the other of *Peter*. By the one, Jesus was lifted up, and by the other, Peter was thrown down; the one makes us pray, and the other makes us blush.

Look at Jesus' trial first. The appearances before Annas and Caiaphas were altogether illegal. It is amazing that a *high* priest could stoop so *low*. At a trial it is expected that a charge will be preferred against the prisoner, but here Jesus is asked questions about himself and his followers (19).

He challenges them to state a case against him, if they can (20, 21); but, so far from being able to do this, they resort to violence (22). That is ever the refuge of cowards. It is more convenient sometimes to strike a face than to state a fact. Nothing is more contemptible than bullying. This is generally done by those who have a surplus of brawn and a minimum of brain.

Compare Jesus' reply to this insult, with Paul's in similar circumstances (23, Acts 23:1-5). What was wanted was argument, not assault; reason, not ruffianism; facts, not fists. Judge war in the light of this principle. The side that has most men and shells generally wins, but that proves nothing. Truth and right are never determined by figures and factories. The conquered are often in the right. Think about that.

● **The trial of Peter** (15-18, 25-27). The other trial is Peter's. He was not taken unawares (13:38), but he had boundless confidence in himself, and for such, nothing but a bad tumble is of any use. We cannot be too sure of God, but we can be overconfident of ourselves. But never despair of a man because he falls. A Pentecost experience can turn a denier into a defender.

Thought: Use your tongue and your teeth for the truth.

John 18:28-40

Pilate and his prisoner

The *civil* trial of Jesus was also in three stages: *before Pilate, before Herod*, and *before Pilate* again. John does not record the second of these. Westcott has pointed out that the trial before Pilate alternates between *without* and *within* the Praetorium, the seven movements (18:28 to 19:16). Of these there are three in this passage: *without* (28-32), where the Jews ask for the death sentence; *within* (33-38a), where Jesus and Pilate talk together; *without* (38b-40), where Pilate declares Jesus innocent. There are also two trials proceeding at the same time, Jesus' and Pilate's. Earlier, Peter, an apostle, was examined by a servant maid, and was found wanting. Now a king is examined by a governor, and the latter fails.

The two most pitiable characters in the gospel story are Judas and Pilate. The one sold his soul to replenish his purse, and the other, to hold his post. Both men had a supreme opportunity, and both lost it. The one was ruined by devilry, and the other by diplomacy.

They brought Jesus to Pilate not for a trial, but for a verdict (29-31). The Jews could pass the death sentence, but they could not execute it (31).

The scene in verses 33-38a is most dramatic. A weak-strong prisoner stands before a strong-weak governor. The latter assumes authority and power; the former has them. One is a subordinate in a kingdom; the other is the sovereign of a kingdom (36,37). One had territory, but the other had truth (37), and these are never of commensurate value.

Some people still mistake property for power, and position for principle. Pilate said, '*I find in him no fault at all—but*'. That was fatal, for Pilate. No reservation should ever be put upon right. Principles are not *pawns* that can at will be sacrificed to save a tottering *castle*. Pilate did not understand that, but he was check-mated at last, as every wrong-doer is.

Thought: He who trifles is asking for trouble.

John 19:1-16

The judge self-judged

The other four alternations are in this passage: *within* the Praetorium (1-3); *without* (4-7); *within* (8-11); *without* (12-16). Mark these in your Bible margin. We cannot reconcile what is here recorded with any semblance of justice. When a decision has been reached the trial does not go on in any court of law. But after Pilate had handed Jesus over to the Jews for death, he tells them that he finds no fault in him (4). No true man wants a verdict based on pity, but only on justice (5). Imagine a governor, presiding over a trial, saying, '*Take ye him, and crucify him: for I find no fault in him.*' Sin dethrones reason, and selfishness dethrones right.

It was not for the civil authorities to pronounce on religious questions (7). How pathetic to hear this impotent man say, '*I have power*' (10). Consider well Christ's reply (11). In a strictly legal sense Pilate had authority, but it was delegated and not inherent. His sin was great, but the High Priest's was greater, the one sinned on a civil level, but the other on a spiritual level; the one against human justice, but the other against divine revelation.

Pilate's conscience is still pulling one way, and his self-interest another way, and his will capitulates to the latter (12-16). What did the Jews care for Caesar, except to hate him, but they readily play the card of a feigned patriotism in order to win their diabolical game (12,15). What a problem this whole thing is!

Had all these people been just, Jesus would never have died, but their injustice remains the blackest crime in history, notwithstanding the fact that the issue of it accomplished the redemption of the world. Not only should we never do evil that good may come, but we shall never get credit for any good that in the providence of God may come of our evil-doing. Right is not a balancing of chances, but adherence to enlightened principle.

Thought: Right should be rigid.

John 19:17-30

Calvary

This portion is the heart of the gospel, the focus of history, the essence of revelation, the crown of wisdom, the criterion of truth, and the foundation of faith. The incomparable event in human history is **the crucifixion of Jesus Christ**. The fact of a crucifixion is not unique, for many both before and after were crucified, and two others at the time, but the meaning of Christ's crucifixion is absolutely unique; it stands forth at once a charge and a challenge.

With the details we are familiar. Three crosses, and Jesus '*in the midst*'. That is always his place; in the midst of *learning* (Luke 2:46); of *devotion* (Matthew 18:20); of *misery* (18); of *bewilderment* (20:19,26); of *testimony* (Revelation 1:13); and of *eternal glory* (Revelation 5:6; 7:17).

Pilate became determined too late (22). Some acts are fatal. One man '*lifted up his eyes in hell*'. He had better long before have lifted them up to heaven. Make sure that you are not too late.

The soldiers did not say and do what is recorded in verses 23,24, that the Scripture might be fulfilled, but the Scripture was fulfilled by their so doing.

Very tender is the solicitude of Jesus, while on the cross, for his mother (25-27). Why did not her other sons take care of her? Think of her living with John at Ephesus.

How significant are the words *accomplished* and *finished* at this time (28,30). Compare 4:34; 5:36; 17:4. The people thought that it was Jesus that was finished, but, in reality, it was the devil, for now he fatally bruised the serpent's head.

Calvary was the fulfilment, at a point of time, of an eternal purpose; it was the embodiment of the character of God, the love that is absolutely holy and perfectly righteous. The cross shows that God is capable of suffering. The death of Jesus is the key to history, and the one hope of the world.

Thought: There is a seeming loss which is eternal gain.

John 19:31-42

The tomb

Seven persons are brought to our notice in this passage. First and chiefly, **Jesus**, now dead. His spirit has departed, and is in the care of God (30). His broken, bleeding body is limply hanging on the tree. To precipitate death the legs of the crucified were sometimes broken, but there was no need in Jesus' case. God never intended that that should be done (36, Exodus 12:46; Numbers 9:12; Psalm 34:20). Mark the precision of verses 36,37. In verse 36, the Scripture referred to was *fulfilled*, that was the end of it; but in verse 37, we read, *'another Scripture saith'*; it does not say *fulfilled*, because Zechariah 12:10 is yet to be fully accomplished (Revelation 1:7).

Then there are the **two thieves** (31). They were not dead, and so suffered the last torture—the one going to Gehenna, and the other, to Paradise.

Once again, and for the last time, we get a glimpse of **Pilate** (38). As he was firm too late with the Jews (22) so he is tender too late with Jesus. Readily he gave up the body for a decent burial, rather than let it be thrown into the common hole. I beseech of you, don't be kind too late.

Could **John** forget these tragic hours? The memory of them was green-fresh after sixty-five years, and he would lovingly go over every detail: *'he that saw it bare record'* (35).

Next, there is **Joseph** of Arimathaea (38), a secret disciple, from fear. How turbulent must have been his emotions now! How he would long that he might have openly confessed Jesus while he was alive! Post-mortem courage is a tearful thing. Be brave while the battle is on.

Finally, there is **Nicodemus** (39,40). His history is in three brief passages: *desire for Christ* (3:1-15); *defence of Christ* (7:45-52), and *devotion to Christ* (here). The growth of a soul.

Think of the grave in the garden, of tragedy in beauty, of death in a setting of delights. It was a fact. It is a parable.

Thought: 'From the ground there blossoms red,
   Life that shall endless be.'

John 20:1-18

The great new beginning

The *trial* (18:12 to 19:16), and the *tragedy* (19:17-42), are followed by the *triumph of divine love* (chapter 20). In this chapter our attention is called to five things: *the great discovery; love rewarded; peace for fear; certainty for doubt;* and *the purpose of the record*.

● **The great discovery** (1-10). It was made by a woman and two men; by a woman who loved much, because she had been forgiven much, and by two men who, more than any other two of the twelve, had a moulding influence on the church of the first century: Peter, at, and some years after, Pentecost, and in his two *Letters*; and John, in supplying the crown of revelation in his *Gospel*, three *Letters*, and the *Apocalypse*.

These three made the great discovery on the never-to-be-forgotten first day of that week. They represent, in order, perplexity, zeal, and love. *Perplexity* cries, 'They have taken away the Lord out of the sepulchre, and we know not where they have laid him' (2). Mary did not expect a resurrection morning. Her devotion was not based on hope. She was living on memory; but her early visit to the tomb was not to go unrewarded. *Zeal* and *love* were rivals that morning. *Love* won the first lap (4), *zeal*, the second lap (5-7), and *love*, the third lap (8). What an experience!

● **Love rewarded** (11-18). And now that faithful woman is about to get the thrill of her life; how richly was her love rewarded (11-18)! She had said at first, *the Lord* (2), but now she says, *my Lord* (13).

How she adored Jesus! Think of it! She wanted to take away his body (15). Where would she have taken it? How could she have done it? She had not thought of these things; love does not calculate; all she wanted was to have it.

One brief word changed all—*Mary*, and her soul answered back with pulsating rapture—*Rabboni, my dear Master* (16). What a millennium of joy was packed into that moment! Do you love him like that?

Thought: The vision is for the devoted.

John 20:19-31

Holy friendship

Of the ten *appearances* of the Lord in resurrection life to his disciples, five were on the day of the resurrection, 'the first day of the week.' Of these five our chapter records the first, to Mary (14-18), and the last, to the assembled disciples in the upper room (19-23). Between these are the appearances to certain women (Matthew 28:8-10), to Peter (Luke 24:34), and to the two disciples on the way to Emmaus (Luke 24:13-31).

● **Peace for fear** (19-23). To the disciples assembled in the evening of that momentous Sunday (19), Jesus gave peace for fear. Is it not strange that they were so held by fear after they had learned that the Master was alive again? Well, Jesus appeared *in the midst* of their bewilderment, and he gave to them indisputable evidence of his identity—*his hands and his side*.

But *peace* was not enough, they needed *power*, and he gave them that also (22). Compare this with the blessing of Pentecost. And what formerly he had given to Peter, he now gave to all the apostles, the spiritual discernment which is authority (23, cf.Matthew 16:19). By and in Christ all his people may have peace, and joy, and power, and authority.

● **Certainty for doubt** (24-29). What follows is the first of the five *appearances* after the resurrection day, eight days after (26), and then Jesus gave certainty for doubt. What infinite condescension and consideration are in Jesus' coming again for the sake of one man who was absent the week before (24). Thomas was not an infidel. He might have become one, but Jesus said, '*Become not* faithless, but believing' (27). By his previous absence he had missed a blessing (29), but he got the next best. You are not like Thomas unless you also can say, '*My Lord and my God.*'

The purpose of the record (31). Verse 31 is the key-verse of the key-book of the Bible. *Faith in the God-Man-Redeemer brings eternal life.* To declare and demonstrate that, this book was written.

Thought: Faith is not dependent on sight.

John 21:1-14

Night and morning

We now come to **the epilogue** (21:1-25) as the last two verses of chapter 20 show. It records the appearance of the risen Lord to seven of his disciples by the lake of Galilee (1,2). In verse 14, John is counting only the appearances '*to the disciples*': to the ten on Easter day, to the eleven a week later, and this one.

Our passage is in two parts.

- **The draught of fishes** (1-8).

What a fraternity is this (2)! Peter, Thomas, Nathanael, James, John, and probably Andrew and Philip. Trace all that is said of these, and we shall readily understand how unique a company they formed in this crisis. The time is between Passover and Pentecost.

Do not assume that Peter and the others did wrong in going *a fishing*. The Lord would not have his people stand idle in between times. Nor are we to conclude that the failure that night was due to any want of faith on the part of these men. Have you ever toiled fruitlessly? Do not be discouraged: the morning and Jesus are at hand (4). He is often close by when we are unaware of his presence. *Right* is not contrasted with *wrong*, but with *left*. What a result (6,11)!

From Augustine on, Luke 5:1-11 and this event have been mystically compared. *That* represents the visible church, containing good and bad: the net is cast without special direction as to side; the net was broken and many escaped. *This* represents God's elect, foreknown by him: all are good; the net is brought to shore, and none are lost. Nothing is so quick as love (7). Zeal follows after (7).

- **The breakfast on the shore** (9-14).

Fire of coals (9) occurs here and in 18:18, only. At the one, Peter thrice denied his Lord; at the other, he thrice confessed him. We should rise where we fall. Before the rebuke (15) came the repast (13). If the question had come first, Peter would have wanted no breakfast. Time your challenges more carefully.

Thought: Failure may quickly be exchanged for success.

John 21:15-25

The end

Jesus remembered. Peter had said, '*Although all shall be offended, yet will not I*' (Mark 14:29). That was a reflection on his brother apostles. Now, after the sad fall, Jesus says, '*Lovest thou me more than these?*' Certainly the reference is to the disciples, and not to the nets or fishes. This reminder which Peter is given of his previous self-confidence leads him to speak modestly of himself in what follows.

Two words are here translated *love*. Jesus asks, 'Dost thou in the full determination of the will, in profound reverence and devotion, love me?' Peter does not say *yes*, but confesses that the Lord is dear to him. This question and that answer are repeated (16), and then Jesus drops his word, and uses Peter's (17a), and it was that which grieved the apostle, and not because the question was put three times (17b).

Following this is Peter's commission (15-17): feed my *lambs* and my *sheep*, the young and the old. The apostle remembered that when he wrote, '*Ye were as sheep going astray; but are now returned unto the shepherd and bishop of your souls*' (1 Peter 2:25).

Now the record is about to terminate, and it does so on the note of the future of Peter and John, intimating that the former would die violently, and the latter naturally, which tradition affirms they did (18-23). We should learn from verse 19 that we can *glorify God* by death as well as by life, and this the martyrs have done.

Let us appreciate Peter's solicitude for his friend (21), for they had been much in one another's company during the preceding sad days; but, nevertheless, Jesus rebuked his curiosity (22). Our interest in one another must never become a substitute for the faithful following of Christ. Verse 23 shows how easily we may misinterpret what Christ says.

Apparently the last two verses were not written by the author of this Gospel: compare *we* and *his* (24).

Thought: Love is the mother and queen of all the virtues.